MIND your own LIFE

MIND your own LIFE

the journey back to love

Aaron Anson

BALBOA.
PRESS

A DIVISION OF HAY HOUSE

Balboa Press books may be ordered through booksellers or by contacting:

Balboa Press
A Division of Hay House
1663 Liberty Drive
Bloomington, IN 47403
www.balboapress.com
1-(877) 407-4847

Because of the dynamic nature of the Internet, any web addresses or links contained in this book may have changed since publication and may no longer be valid. The views expressed in this work are solely those of the author and do not necessarily reflect the views of the publisher, and the publisher hereby disclaims any responsibility for them.

The author of this book does not dispense medical advice or prescribe the use of any technique as a form of treatment for physical, emotional, or medical problems without the advice of a physician, either directly or indirectly. The intent of the author is only to offer information of a general nature to help you in your quest for emotional and spiritual well-being. In the event you use any of the information in this book for yourself, which is your constitutional right, the author and the publisher assume no responsibility for your actions.

Certain stock imagery © Thinkstock. Any people depicted in stock imagery provided by Thinkstock are models, and such images are being used for illustrative purposes only.

ISBN: 978-1-4525-3290-5 (e)
ISBN: 978-1-4525-3289-9 (sc)
ISBN: 978-1-4525-3291-2 (hc)

Library of Congress Control Number: 2011906713

Printed in the United States of America

Balboa Press rev. date: 9/12/2011

This book is dedicated to the memory of gay teenagers and those who gave up or lost their lives in the struggle to find a peaceful existence in a noisy place while longing to have their muted voices heard—and to those embracing a silent love story that cannot be yet told. You are not forgotten.

The lessons within are dedicated to those who desire quieting the hateful rhetoric to behold the peace and blissfulness of our universe.

Table of Contents

Table of Contents

The way we live our lives tells a story . . . a story that affects those around us in profound ways. When I met Aaron, his story was one that not only fascinated me, but one that made me change my own story. His life tells a narrative of love, acceptance, freedom, and happiness. I found it remarkable how he lets go of all expectations of others and fully celebrates who they are—this is the true definition of love. An important creed in his life is how others' happiness is compulsory for his own. His generosity is evident in the way that he gives unconditionally of himself without expecting anything in return. He touched my life with his ability to extract his ego from situations and in return choosing to be kind, rather than right. Aaron Anson chooses a tale that assists him in loving himself, loving others, creating more, and will result in the highest good for everyone involved. When looking at Aaron's life, it is clear that his definition of achievement is indeed self-acceptance. It's easy to obtain material possessions, yet changing your deepest thoughts and learning to love yourself is the true triumph.

Walter Bradley, Psychologist
WalterBradley.com

Acknowledgements

To Sporty Momma for your relentless encouragement and cheerleading on the sidelines. For your many words of wisdom through the years that kept me grounded and proud to be your son. Nothing has driven me more than constantly hearing you say you're proud of me, and that I could do anything. Thanks for your love, your faith, and your encouragement throughout this long and, at times, difficult journey. Your continued prayers of love and support sustained me even though I'd go astray of the way you thought I should. For those times you held your heart in your hand as I scurried about the abysses and pitfalls of life to find my own way, I thank you. I'm eternally grateful to have had you witness this high point in my life that you believed would happen long before I ever knew.

My children Kesha and Aaron, you have been a constant source of inspiration and joy—from the day you were born. You, along with my beautiful grandchildren, have immensely contributed to my bliss at this stage of my life. You make it so rewarding and worthwhile, and it touches me each and every time you call me *dad*. I commend you both for standing up for what you believe—independent of what others may think. You endured the joys and frustrations of watching your dad grow up alongside you. Your constant love and adoration was invaluable to help me stay in check. You are the rock that strengthens.

Thanks for your faith in me, and for allowing me time to grow and embrace my own knowing.

Elizabeth Indianos, my dear friend, I owe you a debt of gratitude for creating such a magnificent book cover. I appreciate your inspiration, following your heart and stepping into this project at precisely the right times. Your involvement ensured that the master plan was carried out, and your wit, insight, and selfless commitment of love helped make this book great. You ensured this project was a success. Oliver and I both are honored to regard you and your husband John Beck among the world's greatest chefs and our most dear and treasured friends.

Carol Page, my personal assistant and my supportive sister, your insistence on presenting me in the best possible way is evident in the kind and selfless acts you perform each day. You gave your all to Oliver and me very early on, and you deserve a standing ovation.

I'd like to offer a gracious acknowledgement to Dr. Wayne Dyer for his spiritual mentorship. You inspired my own creative wisdom so that I may write and inspire others. Your devotion to illuminating the abundance in our lives was just the catalyst I needed to get this project underway.

I'm grateful to my many friends and family members who exuded exceptional love and respect for the process while I was writing, and never complained or felt put aside by my lack of availability. Thanks for all the kudos, well wishes, and acts of kindness from those who offered congratulations and support. I came to realize an even deeper understanding of gratitude for those who could have chosen to stifle enthusiasm, but instead chose to selflessly offer their excitement, along with their friendship and love. With regret to those I've forgotten to mention, who have made many other selfless contributions on this journey, I ask your forgiveness and offer you my most sincere gratitude and love.

Above all, I personally express my love and sincerest gratitude to my biggest fan, friend, and partner Oliver. You have been a tremendous beacon of inspiration in my life. You made me aware of the magnificence of the universe. You are a man of few words, but abundant talent and unfaltering commitment. Your grateful poise and your outlook on life redefined my own aspirations and ideals, and your passion in living life beyond pitfalls and setbacks ignited my soul and set my dormant desires afire.

I apologize for your having to sit patiently beside me through many flights, having to be entertained by talkative passengers and your iPod as I scribbled notes on the back of in-flight napkins or tapped away on the keyboard of Bunky (my laptop), trying to preserve thoughts that hurried through my head.

Your faith and patience in allowing me to grow is an extraordinary accomplishment all by itself. If for no other reason, I'll always love you, just because. I am fortunate and profoundly grateful to have you as my technical editor and my chief critic. I admire your commitment to quality even when I was defiant. Your ability to help communicate my ideas to others will never go unappreciated, and I regret you are not editing this part of the book.

Special thanks to you and Expert Mac Repair for setting up our highly acclaimed website, so that others may become aware of what we were doing and participate as they have.

Lastly, I am forever grateful for your showing me that unconditional love and dedication really does exist. I am humbled by your spirit and truly blessed to share your friendship, your companionship, and, most of all, your love.

Let us spend one day as deliberately as Nature, and not be thrown off the track by every nutshell and mosquito's wing that falls on the rails . . . If the engine whistles, let it whistle till it is hoarse for its pains. If the bells rings, why should we run? . . . I have always been regretting that I was not as wise as the day I was born.

Henry David Thoreau

Self-thinkers: individualized, intentional, independent, intuitive; thinking without confirmation or approval from others.

This definition sums up my reason for writing this entire book, which is meant to encourage a deeper exploration of the human experience.

I hope to foster a transcendent dialogue on the human spirit and its relationship with our beliefs. It is not my intention to disparage any religion or religious belief, but I do call into question any church's philosophy that claims to have all the answers, but doesn't ask any crucial questions. I challenge doctrines and teachings that have been blindly passed down for thousands of years, without being widely questioned. I ask why we believe as we do, and how we arrived at those beliefs. I'll even explore the path not taken that would have led us to different beliefs.

Although it's awkward and void of inspiration, at times I may come across as critical of those Christians I feel stray from our highest calling: unconditional love.

However complex it may seem, my quest has been to communicate on a level above our senses of sight, hearing, smell, and touch in order to transcend our ordinary level of awareness and connect with our originating Source. Once we reconnect with our Source, we can then establish the moment our beliefs—about morality, sexuality, abortion, racism, and more—were formed. We'll even discover why we believe the way we do, and how our superiority complexes evolved.

Shall we then dare to go one step further and cultivate our most valuable resource: our own minds? And if we squander this birthright by living our entire existence based on the desires, values, and beliefs perpetuated by others, who is responsible?

Throughout this writing, I have refrained as much as possible from quoting biblical scriptures to validate my points. I am acutely aware that scriptures, much like a movie, a conversation, or even this book, are open to interpretation, and I see no value in adding one more to the countless Biblical interpretations out there. I've always been fascinated with the life and teachings of Jesus, Buddha, Confucius, Gandhi, and many other spiritual teachers. I have no interest in proving or disproving any of their sacred teachings—I merely want to call attention to the necessity of seeking our own truth, as well, and ascertaining that we are not beholden to someone else's truth.

Many times the Bible is used as a weapon—to falsely embolden our own beliefs and force them upon others. If we look back at the Civil War, we'll see that the North and the South both used the same Bible to defend their points of view and justify their reasons for fighting the war. Southern preachers took certain parts of the Bible literally, using scriptures to defend slavery: "slaves, obey your earthly masters with fear and trembling" and "tell slaves to be submissive to their masters and to give satisfaction in every respect."[1] Northern preachers, on the other hand, were confident that God was on their side. The words of The Battle Hymn of the Republic summed up their belief: "as He died to make men holy, let us die to make men free." They would even cite the book of Revelations to suggest that if the North won the Civil War, it might pave the way for a kingdom of God here on earth. You have

---

1   Ephesians 6:5 and Titus 2:9.

to wonder if the same misinterpretation is still happening with today's hot social issues, like abortion and marriage equality.

I used as my guides some of the greatest spiritual teachers, such as Jesus and Buddha. Notably, they themselves never wrote anything down. Instead, their less distinguished followers would perform the task of recording their teachings for others to read. I conclude, as some others have too, that the leaders themselves never wrote because they felt that written language couldn't maintain the integrity of their message.

Consider this: the Old Testament in the Christian Bible is based on the Tanakh, the Hebrew Bible. It has been altered throughout to support the teachings of Christianity instead of Judaism. Even more, there are now many versions of the Christian Bible, each one choosing different translations of various words to express what the translation's authors felt were most important or most accurate.

Given that the Bible alone has several interpretations, not writing things down would have ensured the original message of inspiration remained consistent with its source, thus restraining multiple interpretations from being made out of the original intended context. This is evident in the countless interpretations we are inundated with today—all alleging to be precise.

First and foremost, I have to acknowledge that regardless of what others decipher or interpret, we have a far superior interpreter at our own disposal that is perfectly aligned to our wellbeing in the universe. I chronicle my life experiences and offer deliberate dialogue based on my reasoning—however not withstanding debate. It would be ignorant on my part to disregard this innate awareness and ability for each of us to examine our own reasoning capacity individually. Furthermore it would be contemptuous to convey this absolute privilege of discernment to anyone else to subjectively instruct my soul's existence within the universe.

This book is not about changing one's mind, but rather engaging one's mind. My endeavor is to inspire you to rise above the persuasive rhetoric of politics, preaching, and even philosophy. My truths and experiences should serve only as a precedent. You can then seek and find your own truths within this cosmic creation, the universe. The catalyst for the confirmation we seek may be through, Buddhism, Christianity, Islam, or other teachings—or combinations thereof—so it is important that our minds be open to all things and not attached to any one thing. Only then can your enlightenment give birth to your own self-affirmation.

I'm but a minuscule fraction of matter that is cooperatively working together with every other minute fraction of matter to facilitate the workings of the universe as a whole. Until the day I see clouds criticizing, rain condemning, trees arguing, stars boasting, air attacking, the moon molesting, or the sun despising—I will hold to a fundamental belief that everyone and everything God created is good precisely the way it was created! Anything shy of this opposes good (or God) and is incapable of being in harmony with the originating Source that created it.

PART I
ENLIGHTENMENT

The earth is mind-bendingly old: 4.54 billion years old, according to researchers and geologists. In fact, the earth was around for 117 million years before the moon formed. Upon hearing of these massive time spans, an inquisitive person might ask about our lives here on earth: "Where was I when all this was taking place," "Where am I right now," and, "Where will I be in the future?"

Nobody on earth can know the answers to questions like these, so I certainly won't pretend to. But let's ponder briefly: where were you and I one hundred years ago? How about one thousand, or even one billion years ago? Surely we were indeed *somewhere* in the universe. Even more perplexing, where will you and I be a million years from today?

Our bodies weigh exactly the same before and after our last breath[2]. It's reasonable to say that we are much more than our bodies, which are really just a vessel for our experience here on earth. Our minds define who we truly are. You might even say that we're never actually in our bodies to begin with. But if life has no weight or substance to it,

---

2   In 1907, a physician named Duncan MacDougall weighed people and animals immediately before and after death. He recorded that humans lose about an ounce upon death, but that animals' weights remain the same. He took this to show that humans, but not animals, actually had tangible souls. However, his "study" was poorly controlled, and every study since has shown that people weigh the same before and after death.

then what is it? This is another question that can't be answered here on earth; nevertheless, this notion warrants further inquiry.

These questions beckon us to heighten our awareness of our Source and ask: what, then, gives value to life as we know it? Life has to be contained in our minds, souls, and spirits, since it has no material value. That said, the mind is of utmost importance. Our bodies along with our brains are here in physical form, but our minds are our ultimate observers. The mind exists in all places at once, much as a radio station emits from a remote location but yet is accessible virtually anywhere for those who choose to tune in.

Our material bodies are made up of the exact same matter as were people who came long before us. Their bodies have since decomposed to become part of the earth's surface that we walk on, which in turn, nourishes more plants and animals. Of course, someday our bodies will enter this same cycle.

We are not these physical bodies that we have been taught to believe we are. We are our minds.

Edgar Mitchell, the astronaut pilot of Apollo 14, was one of the first men to walk on the moon. He gave an intriguing account of his experience in space, describing his view out into the great abyss of the universe from his spacecraft. He described galactic clusters, twinkling stars, and limitless cellular formations.

Imagine his powerful epiphany when he sensed that the molecules of his body, the spacecraft, and his flight partners were all connected in a oneness, and that oneness had been prototyped ages ago. Edgar Mitchell's account of his epiphany in space still send chills down my spine:

> Suddenly, from behind the rim of the moon, in long, slow-motion moments of immense majesty, there emerges a sparkling blue and white jewel, a light,

delicate sky-blue sphere laced with slowly swirling veils of white, rising gradually like a small pearl in a thick sea of black mystery. It takes more than a moment to fully realize this is Earth . . . home.

My view of our planet was a glimpse of divinity.

Buddhism has a name for this experience: "samadhi," the highest form of meditation in which you experience oneness with the universe.

After retiring from the astronaut program, Dr. Mitchell founded the Institute of Noetic Sciences: a foundation to sponsor research on consciousness and inner knowing.

Mitchell's experience is compelling, and it's relevant to our lives here on earth today. Such a major paradigm shift has the tendency to put our problems into perspective.

Many times, those we idolize the most are the least perfect. Religious zealots publicly oppose abortion and same-sex marriages, but behind closed doors, they fornicate, divorce and remarry, masturbate, and are unfaithful. When they take these loud, aggressive, hypocritical stances, it only separates us in our journey to achieve a harmonious existence.

It's time for us to become the judges of our own lives.

In our attempt to elevate our standing in society, we insist on separating others into classes by age, race, gender, education, sexual orientation, neighborhoods, income, religion, and every other category we can imagine. We've become obsessed with status, power, and money. We often lose sleep worrying about keeping up with the Joneses, who in turn lose sleep themselves as they try to keep us with us.

We play mind games with the very people we profess to love. Think of all the times you may have been hell-bent on winning an argument with your significant other! We must even evaluate our relationships with those we see on a day-to-day basis.

Perhaps in a hundred or a thousand years, none of these things will really matter.

As we work to make our lives more harmonious, let's remember a quote by Albert Einstein: "We can't solve problems by using the same kind of thinking we used when we created them." Surely, we can take what Einstein said and apply it to our lives today. By using a different kind of thinking, we can answer our questions about spirituality, morality, sexuality, and religion; we can discover the authentic love and acceptance that we once knew.

Welcome to Mind Your Own Life.

Before we were born, we completely submitted the entire first nine months of our lives to our Source. We innately trusted this Source to take the utmost care of us while our hearts, brains, eyes, ears, and hair took shape. Miraculously, all of this form took place from a speck of matter hardly visible, even with a microscope. Now, be aware that all of this happened without input or interference from us, and look at the perfect being that resulted—you.

This brings me to *remembering*. Let's bring awareness to the moment when we stopped surrendering to this Source we had trusted so intimately for the very first nine months of our lives. At what point did ego creep in and we decide to forfeit this birthright? If we are honest, we will acknowledge that the moment we first felt fear, anger, hate, envy, jealousy, or separation, we had disconnected from the Source to which we initially submitted. Our goal now should be to reconnect—without hesitation—and submit once again to the Source we once knew.

Though it should really be nameless, I use *God* and *Source* interchangeably to satisfy our human insistence on giving everything a name. You are free to call it *Spirit*, *God*, or *Source*—whatever you feel most comfortable with. Just understand that words are just words: the word *sun* will not burn you or make you hot any more than the word *cold* will make you need your jacket. It's not the name we give something that gives it meaning.

For future reference, I often link the terms *awareness, knowing, Source,* and *remembering* because they are all necessary for explaining this reconnection to our originating birthright. I also used the word *reconnect* (as opposed to *connect*) because I feel we're all innately connected to Source and could never be completely separated. However, through our learned behavior and prejudices, we experience shorts in this circuitry, and therefore a disrupted flow of our Source energy. To reconnect, we must cleanse our corroded connections so we can reconnect with our birthright—the love we once inherently knew at birth.

There was an incident, when I was thirteen years old, that stands out in my mind as an example of taught hate and prejudice. As a teenager, I would often wear a cap to school; during class I would take it off and place it on the top corner of my desk. One day, a white female classmate of mine walked up from behind me and snatched the cap off my desk, then proceeded to walk away. I stood up in the center row aisle and demanded she give it back. She turned around and began waving the cap in my face, shouting, "Nigger! Nigger! Nigger!"

I tried to snatch the hat back, but she just pulled it back toward her. In a flash, I grabbed her by her hair and elbowed her in the top of the head. The teacher, now aware of the confrontation, intervened to separate us. She got hurt and I got my hat back.

Needless to say, we were both escorted to the principal's office.

—✳︎—

A few weeks later, we found ourselves in court. Her parents had decided that they would sue for the medical expenses of her visit to the doctor and her eyeglasses that got broken during the fight. Because we did not have much money, mom was forced to make a huge financial sacrifice in order to retain an attorney to represent me in court. My attorney pointed out to the judge that I had been a straight-"A," honor roll student up until this incident, and that I had not even one disciplinary action taken against me in school.

The judge asked me to tell my account of the events that took place and led up the altercation, and I did so. He then asked for her side of the story and while sobbing immensely she bawled to tell him "I only called him nigger once!" Angered by her reply and unsympathetic to her crying the judge sternly admonished her," I don't care how many times you said it! the point is you should not have said it even once." He went on to rule that the attack had been provoked by her and explained that the District Attorney had requested that I pay half of her Doctor's bill, but in light of the circumstance, he would not ask me to pay even that. Furthermore he stated that since I was a juvenile the entire case would be expunged from the court records.

I found out years later from a mutual classmate that my antagonist had in fact had a huge crush on me and started out really just wanting my attention. She instinctively loved me but was so easily provoked to hate me. At twelve or thirteen years old she had already been taught to hate and label others with offensive terms. Her family was obviously just as poor as mine as they qualified for a public defender, but somehow she'd been taught to correlate my being black with the word *nigger*, and that it was hateful. On the other hand, I'd learned to accept labels others placed on me.

As tragic as this story seem with the time and monies lost by both our families, and the tremendous sacrifices my mother made to afford me the best defense—this is truly an example of the human capacity to simulate its source and naturally love, and our human ability to forcibly hate.

Let's take a look at a newborn baby so we can better understand our connection to our original Source. Better yet, think of when we ourselves were newborn babies.

Now let's focus on our state of awareness the moment after we were born. At that point we had absolutely no prejudices whatsoever, no hate for anything or anyone. We did not care that our parents were of a particular race, creed, or size. We wouldn't have cared if they were a dreadful dictator or a benevolent champion of human rights. All we knew was that we were in infinite care. Our initial instinct is to love without any preconceived notions—without choice or prejudice.

This awareness is a major shift from our current perception: that we're all somehow different and separate from each other. We've learned to define others by race, sex, height, weight, religion, sexual orientation, and every other category we can imagine. These differences between us are most prevalent in our minds. To shift our thinking and our awareness, we need to observe the larger reality of the universe.

For example, we don't think how different the oranges are that made our orange juice, even if the oranges came from different trees. They may have grown in different states or different countries, or even be of different species! But when the oranges are squeezed, they all produce orange juice, and it is good. It becomes easy to see there's not much more difference between you and me, in the scheme of the entire universe, than there is between two oranges.

The universe is the very body of God, and it is from this body that we were born: perfect, loving, and forgiving, and just as accepting as the stars or the moon. Realizing the beauty of our natural state of love makes you wonder where we got the idea that we are somehow superior (or inferior) to others because of our race, color, creed, or even our ethics and morality. We learned—we were taught—these prejudices, attitudes and behaviors; this wasn't anything we were born with.

That's right! Every prejudice we have against another person was taught to us after we were born. From an infantile state of inherent love, one has to learn to hate, or to feel superior to others. Every single prejudice that a person adopts, every act of resistance to the universe, has to be learned from an outside source—because our most natural state of being is love and acceptance! Our defining moment came when we were birthed from spirit into a material world of physical existence.

Since this is the case, and because we know God as our originating Source, our objective must now be to get back to our Source. This is most certainly an attainable goal, since our Source is our genesis and therefore has always been a part of us. The detrimental behavior we've learned has only kept us separated from fully knowing God and ensured our connection to our Source remains corroded. Our challenge is to unlearn the behaviors that separate us from our Source.

In order to justify our prejudices against each other, we sometimes try to divide Source by declaring that God loves some and hates others. The moment we attempt to do so, our idea of Source is no longer a oneness, but a false duality created to satisfy our egotistical urge to paint others as inferior and ourselves superior. When we act upon these learned prejudices, we completely resist our original Source.

But there is hope that we can relearn. We know how beliefs affect our behavior, and we also know how beliefs can change. People once believed that earth was the center of the universe and the world was flat: if you were to traverse the ocean, you'd fall off into the abyss at some point. Many people in my lifetime believed they'd never witness a black President of the United States. Of course, that notion has been shattered, as well. The fact that many of our once-steadfast beliefs have changed suggests that we can unlearn the destructive belief patterns that we still hold onto today. Our challenge is to rediscover the authentic love we all once knew, instead of relying on the beliefs handed down to us from others.

On a hot Sunday morning in June 1982, my uncle dropped me off at the Savannah airport for an early flight to New York. I had decided it was finally time to go up there and retrieve my customized van—another uncle had talked me into loaning it to him for a week to drive to New York. It was now several weeks later, and all I seemed to be getting from him were weekly promises that he would return it.

It was the trip driving back from New York that would have an immeasurable impact on my life.

Twenty-two years old and having already had a brief stint in the Army, my life was chock full of anxiety and uncertainty. I had acquired a couple of used cars that I repaired and then re-sold for profit, and I got in the rhythm of selling whatever car I was driving to turn a fast buck. Working down at my relatives' salvage yard made this part-time hustle a natural thing to do. I relentlessly toiled to try and find my place in the world—to make my own mark for success.

Much of my striving was done out of fear of being broke, or even destitute. I was frightened when I would see older adults on the streets who were homeless, begging those who passed by. It annoyed me to see relatives constantly complaining about paying their bills. I became feverishly consumed with justifying my own worth not just to myself, but especially to others who doubted me. I felt that the opinions of my family and friends defined me, so I craved their acknowledgement. I was greedy, in a relentless pursuit of money, and I was willing to do whatever it took to feed my obsession—even if it meant buying homes and cars I could not afford, getting married, and burning the candle at both ends by feverishly working.

I sought after and demanded respect from others to define me in lieu of my own self-approval. I did not care about the cost of this achievement, was willing to pay any price for it, and subsequently did.

Reluctantly, my uncle in New York finally agreed to pick me up at the airport after I had waited several hours. It became clear to me that he was having his own struggles in life, and that he wasn't ready to relinquish my van because it was his only transportation.

I arrived in New York City around 8:30 am, but it was close to noon before he retrieved me. He then insisted that I allow him even more time to finish some unattended business he needed to resolve before I took off with his only mode of transportation. He had always carried himself with an aura of success that I and others envied, so it was shocking to see him in this desperate situation.

At 9 PM that night, he finally relinquished my vehicle and I immediately got on the road back to Savannah. I was exhausted from running around the whole day with my uncle, and the traffic and tollbooths in New York gave me some real anxiety. When I finally hit New Jersey, I was relieved. I was traveling south on Interstate 95, when at around three o'clock in the morning near the town of Rocky Mount, I fell asleep at the wheel. I was abruptly awakened when I hit the grass in the center median.

I awoke to the most horrific fear and panic I'd ever experienced. My spontaneous reflex to yank the steering wheel caused me to overcorrect and the van veered back toward the rain-slick highway. The van uncontrollably careened across the road at 75 miles an hour or more, directly to the other side of the highway. After hitting a trench, the van became airborne and whirled some two hundred feet into the thick brush, landing on its side with me inside without a seat belt[3]. Although I was bloodied, I was able to walk out through the broken windshield when I stood up on the driver's door that was on the ground. It was surreal.

I tramped some two hundred feet through the thick brush barefoot; I had managed to lose my shoes in the accident. I made my way up to the side of the highway. Traffic was sparse, and drivers were not able to see the van because it was so far off to the side of the road. Even with the headlights and taillights still on, several vehicles passed, their drivers unaware of the accident. Finally after a few attempts I was able to wave down a passing trucker who summoned the highway patrol.

The next thing I remember was sitting in the passenger seat of the patrol car while the patrolman wrote up an accident report. I will never forget his words, still ringing in my head from that day until this day. "You're actually still alive," he kept repeating in utter amazement, as he shook his head in disbelief.

He told me he had been prepared to call the coroner as soon as he arrived on the accident scene. "You're sitting here and talking to me," he said again in disbelief. After much assurance on my part that I did not want an ambulance, he agreed I didn't need one. Other than massive soreness, amazingly I had only received some scratches, a scrape on my forehead, and several splinters in my feet from trudging through the underbrush without shoes.

There are not many days that the trooper's words don't echo in my head, and this makes me aware again that I am still here, still talking, and still breathing. In retrospect, I realized that my daughter had been

---

3   During this time there were no laws requiring seat belt use, and it was not even taught in the drivers' education class I had taken in high school.

conceived two weeks prior to the accident. She would become a much-needed source of joy in my life eight-and-a-half months later. That day could very well have been the last day of my earthly existence; yet for a higher and divine purpose, I was spared and left to tell.

When I was a young boy, I didn't even consider the possibility that I was gay; for one thing, I didn't have the language for it. What I learned in Sunday school was that for a boy, acting feminine was bad and unchristian. I didn't know anything else about being gay, about boys being attracted to other boys or men to other men. My parents never discussed gay relationships—they simply were denied to even exist at all. I had no idea what gay relationships were.

And yet, there was something inside me that knew. And the part of me that knew was very afraid. For years as a young boy, I had a recurring nightmare about a devil creature with horns that would come to poke me with his pitchfork and then laugh as I bled profusely in the bed. I tried to scream for my mother, who was sleeping in the next room, but my screams were muffled as I felt my breath smothered. Even though I wasn't conscious of the connection, I knew in the deepest part of myself that this dream was connected to the feelings I had for other boys—to my own nascent, unspoken, unexpressed homosexual feelings.

But the world I grew up in had no room for such things, and as I got older and became more aware of my conflicting feelings, I wondered if anyone else felt these things. At barbecues with all the extended family, surrounded by the excited shouts of my cousins and the laughter of my aunts and uncles, breathing in the smell of hamburgers on the grill, I would wonder if I was the only one in this huge group who felt what I felt.

While there was no discussion of sexual orientation—that term itself would have been laughable—sometimes someone would make a crack with the word "fag" or "sissy," and I'd feel my face go hot with an unnameable shame, even though I thought those were just terms for people who didn't behave right, and who were in some mysterious way "bad." In my simple view, if you didn't want to burn in hell for acting like a girl, you just shouldn't act like a girl.

At age seventeen, I joined the military, feeling that I had overcome the worst of my gay tendencies. I had resisted all the urges and I had repented for the bad thoughts that would not go away. I hoped the military would finish my transition from boyhood into manhood while making me a bona fide saint as well—or at least that the rules and regulations of the military would provide even more restrictions on my behavior than I could provide by myself. When the recruiter asked me if I was gay, I emphatically said no, for even at that point I did not know what *gay* was. My definition would have been a guy who acts like a girl, or who wishes he was a girl. I still hadn't realized that my attraction to other men would be described with the same "gay" word I used for guys who acted like girls.

My answer satisfied the recruiter. Soon I was leaving my hometown and boarding a Greyhound bus for a several hour drive up to Jacksonville, Florida, where we would have our medical exams and orientation.

Once we got to the military medical reception center, all of us new recruits were herded like cattle, off of the bus and into single file to get our first physical exam for our entry into the military.

Up until then, I had effectively suppressed my same-sex attraction to the point where it had been manageable. I had been confident that I had my masculinity firmly under control. But then I found myself in this huge room like an auditorium, in a group of forty or so other guys. We were told to form a circle facing each other, and we were ordered to strip bare naked for the first part of our exam. We all looked aimlessly around the room, trying not to acknowledge each other's private parts, but with so many male genitalia flopping all over the place it was hard not to take notice of all the many shapes and sizes. Meanwhile, a couple of doctors went around the circle, sticking their gloved fingers up each of our butts while asking us to bend over and cough. This was the first part of the medical exam.

Next, they asked us to put our underwear back on and then to stand, nearly naked, in a single file to receive the first in a series of shots we would need in order to be fully accepted into the military. They made us line up so the doctor could get his electronic shot gun and shoot each of us in the shoulder as we were ushered, one behind the other, into a much smaller room nearby. Of course, we all inched backward from the guy in front, so as not to appear gay or girlish in any way. We wouldn't want to be so close to another guy's rear end with only underwear on! That would not last long, because a drill sergeant policing the line shouted very authoritatively, "Nuts to butts, guys; tighten this line up!" The shouting continued: "This is not your mother, these are your comrades here!" Before long, there was a sense of comfort in having some guy's privates nearly touching yours, of being in close proximity to the next guy's butt—because we were ordered to. This situation was a major test of my commitment to my manhood. It was the first experience in my adulthood to see how other guys behaved with each other when they are vulnerable, with their sexuality exposed.

Needless to say, I was relieved to see that day of moral testing draw to a close. But my relief was short-lived, because soon I was off to basic training, having to share communal showers, and bunking down with several other guys. Victoriously, I made it through basic training and advanced training without incident, and I was moved on to my permanent duty station in Ft. Campbell, Kentucky.

I found my experience at Ft. Campbell new and exciting. I had looked forward to not using communal showers and bunking with other guys, as I needed all the help I could get in resisting my attraction to the other men. But my euphoric sensation would not last long. My first morning as a new Private on base, I was shown to the mess hall. While in line requesting how I wanted my eggs cooked, I was approached by a sergeant in the kitchen asking if he could meet me later for dinner, off-base somewhere. I remember knowing intuitively what he was after. I politely declined his invitation. I was seventeen, away from home and from all those who had a foothold in my religious upbringing. For the very first time in my life, I felt leeway to make my own independent decisions. But those deeply rooted fears of religious persecution would continue to haunt me and not allow me room to bend—even a bit—to my inner desires.

About a week later, I was asked to pull a twenty-four hour guard duty shift outside our barracks, and I was joined by a fellow soldier who was on duty as well. During the course of conversation, he invited me over to his place to have beers for a guy's night out. He said that his wife, who happened to be a sergeant in the military as well, would be pulling an overnight guard duty, and that their children would be staying with friends.

I was eager to make friends in my new environment, and I readily agreed to join him. It was the perfect welcome I needed: a married guy with kids and experience in the military, who could show me the ropes and introduce me to military and adult life . . . or so I thought.

I arrived at my newfound friend's off-base apartment, and he generously offered me beer, as promised. I listened to the small talk he made about life in the military. The evening gave way, rather quickly, to him asking me to relax a bit and spend the night if I liked, because his wife would not be home that evening anyway. I was nervous, but without inhibition. I took the bait, thinking I had found a cool new friend. I thought there was no way that a married man—especially one in the military—would be interested in having sex with me. And even as all this was rushing through my head, and even though I found myself wishing that I was wrong, I kept feeling the tug of the ropes that anchored me to my religious upbringing that was completely intolerant of homosexuals. I was just barely aware of my sexual desires, yet I deeply felt I had to suppress those desires—because of my inherited religious beliefs.

Eventually, he must have thought I was relaxed enough, or that I had caught onto the fact that he was interested in having sex with me. When he began to caress my hand, I froze in panic. My heart prepared to jump out of my chest. But I did not run or even move, since the affectionate touch wasn't all that bad, either. I asked myself over in over in my head, "How did I get into this situation?" Yes, I felt a sexual attraction from the start, but this was a safe bet, I thought! The guy's married, he's in the military, and he has three kids for God's sake!

I devised a plan to leave, and I got out before anything could happen. That was just my first experience with the real world where some guys were interested in other guys. As it turned out, the sexual advances like this would not let up. It was as though I'd actually signed up for a "scared straight" boot camp to challenge my ability to resist my sexual temptations. My attraction toward guys was very real and not attached to sex at all since I had no interest in sex, just an intimacy with a guy.

There goes the theory some politicians have that banning gays in the military is effective. Not to mention, this was over thirty years ago.

After first going through many sleepless nights of turmoil and confusion, I spent the next several months making countless trips to the chaplain on base for spiritual guidance—to no avail. He referred me to a military psychiatrist, and I was eventually diagnosed with bouts of depression and bouts of high anxiety; they called it "bipolar disorder." These problems would last for another twenty years or more, off and on.

Ten months later, I was honorably discharged from the military because of my chronic conditions. I went back south to bounce between the small Florida town where I grew up and Savannah, Georgia, where I had other relatives. I took odd jobs like carpenter's helper and construction laborer, and I eventually ended up working for my uncles in the auto salvage business. I only hoped now that no one would ask and I'd never have to tell anyone about my struggling transition into manhood.

My immediate reaction was to immerse myself in every religious service I could find. For every big preacher who came to town, for every tent revival, I would drop everything just so I could attend. I bounced around among the Pentecostal, Baptist, and Methodist churches. I even briefly followed the Jehovah's Witness, Seventh Day Adventist, and Mormon churches. I was baptized more times than I can remember. I was so fascinated with being told how to live, I suppose. I was elected and appointed to deacon boards, financial and prayer committees, and the list goes on for each church I joined. My obsession with being a good Christian would prove futile: I had retreated back to the South after my stint in the military—right back to where all the brainwashing had begun. Even immersed in the church community, I was not sheltered from constant sexual undercurrents and propositions from men, often from church leaders and parishioners who were married to saintly sisters of the church.

My own homosexual prejudices had now come full circle. My faith had taught me to abhor myself. At seventeen, everything I had been made to believe and taught to emulate about the military and the church were shattered beyond recognition. I found no redemptive value in denying myself, just to uphold the egotistical desires of those with religious or secular influence.

A day of full reckoning would be further down the road for me yet, as I would still struggle with my sexual identity for another eighteen years. For I had a twofold battle now: that of being accepted in the Southern Bible belt as being both gay and black.

My father died suddenly from a stroke a couple weeks after I turned ten. My mother was left to raise eleven children alone with the youngest only five. Even without my dad, I grew up in a close and loving family surrounded by many other relatives and family friends—who all had a profound influence on my life.

We were poor but proud, as my mother took on several jobs to help support us, barely keeping us off welfare. She would always end up taking traditionally masculine occupations, as jobs for guys usually paid more than jobs for women. As a result, she did mechanic and auto body work on cars, and drove buses or tractor-trailers to help make ends meet.

I was brought up going to Sunday school and church every Sunday. Growing up with such a large family in a three-bedroom, one-bathroom house made going to church something to look forward to for space if nothing else. I became so fascinated with church that I found myself emulating the preacher and the Sunday school teacher. Me and my siblings would set up mock pulpits in our back yard. My brothers and I would take turns being the preacher and the others would be our members.

Eventually, I found myself joining a little Pentecostal church out on the edge of town. Here, I was allowed to become a preacher at just twelve years old. I would read my Bible for hours each day, and I even took it to school with me: badgering my classmates with sermons they had no interest in hearing. I would carry to school a briefcase full of religious tracts, that promised hell and damnation, and I would hand them out to other twelve-year-olds.

The other youth preachers and I would beg the church overseer to let us preach the message on Sunday. I'd look forward to giving the members and elders of the church a chance to shout and dance about in a lively praise worship. My preaching conveniently concealed my nascent attraction to guys as well by allowing me to openly condemn homosexuals from the pulpit (although I did not fully know what homosexuality was). It felt so rewarding when members would comment, after the service, on what a swell job I had done in preaching and making them feel the Holy Ghost.

My closest influences were these super-religious church folks and my family, so my views and beliefs were based largely on the examples they set for me.

Unfortunately, the examples that stuck with me most were set by those who used money as a form of power and influence against others. From those around me, I learned to define *power* as the ability to manipulate others and master others' perceptions of me.

To be considered successful, one would have to out-charm the other by any means necessary. Some would buy newer or faster cars, or larger and prettier houses than the others—mostly for the bragging rights that came along with them. The public declaration of success was bestowed upon whoever was perceived to have the most money—and therefore the most power—and that recognition was envied by the others. This was all I'd ever known or been exposed to, and so it made sense that I would follow the examples set before me.

At the same time, little emphasis was ever placed on becoming a more decent individual. The subtle teachings of my family and others would certainly encourage one to become a more pretentious person. Their *modus operandi* was to deceive—faking it before actually making it so as to discourage others.

It was very alluring, this promise of getting so much envy and social mileage from material achievements. The whole system of manipulation helped to foster my reckless thinking and behavior very early in life. When I began my elusive quest for money and wealth, it seemed hardly out of the ordinary. But later, I would harbor resentment for being taught that money, power, and buying a large square box called a house were good, and would somehow make me a good person and an accomplished American.

In their defense, most of my ancestors and family grew up in the South: Florida, Georgia and Alabama, during a period when discrimination was blatantly supported by law. For generations, most of my ancestors had been denied many of the basic human rights I enjoy today. Many were alive during a time when hate-based laws prevented whites from marrying blacks and allowed whites to actually purchase blacks. There were laws which mandated that blacks were really only three-fifths of a person, and that white human beings could buy and own black human beings. The constant struggle to survive, both financially and emotionally, must have been a heavy burden for many of them to bear.

Being some of these hate-based, discriminatory laws just came off the books within my lifetime, I can only imagine how my life would have been had I been born only a decade earlier. As late as 1967, the Chief of Police in Sarasota, Florida was authorized to clear any public beach if members of different races were present. In 1963, Birmingham, Alabama mandated that if a business had both black and white employees, they must maintain separate bathrooms. Even today, laws remain that exhibit prejudice against immigrants, prevent gays from serving in the military, prevent same sex unions, and disallow abortions. But these too will change. Eventually, we'll regard these laws as the cruel inequities of the past because love will always conquer hate.

Even though, by the time I came on the scene, my family was not in such dire straits as my ancestors, their fear of poverty and their fear of lack remained. As a form of compensation, they felt that they must amass material possessions to improve their lives beyond those before them. It's certainly comprehensible how, after experiencing denial for so long, greed could result. Even so, many spent so much time focusing on greed that they were never able to achieve material abundance in their lives. Although it was a long time ago that I was surrounded by these behaviors, I have to be aware that my learned behavior from my past, occasionally, tries to resurface in my life today.

*Flowers are without hope. Because hope is tomorrow
and flowers have no tomorrow.*

Antonio Porchia

When I was a young man, I valued money a lot more than I do today. When I was twenty-two, I lent some money to one of my aunts, and as time went on, I felt a mounting resentment at her failure to pay me back. Finally, I lost it: I was at work one day and got word that my aunt was denying the debt. Infuriated, I walked off the job without even clocking out and I drove to her house.

I pulled in front of her house in a fury and got out of the car. As I walked toward the doorstep, she and her live-in boyfriend came out of their house to confront me in the front yard. She was armed with a rifle, aimed right at my face. They kept on walking toward me until the end of the rifle was within a foot of my nose.

By this time, I was so enraged that I begged them to shoot me if they'd dare! In the heat of the moment, I completely forgot I had a wife, a young daughter, and a newborn all waiting for me at home on the other side of town. With my egotistical temper, my will to die that day was stronger than my willingness to live or retreat. Though she tried repeatedly, she couldn't get the gun to shoot. As her boyfriend looked on, my aunt started shouting obscenities while attempting to load a bullet in the chamber of her firearm. Adrenaline pumping through my veins, my ego had taken over and I reciprocated with obscenities of my own. In disgust, she shouted: "This fucking thing won't shoot!" She then grabbed it by the barrel and started to beat me in the head with the butt of the rifle while her boyfriend, a very muscular guy, rushed over to restrain me with a bear hug.

After struggling and breaking free, and even more enraged, I ran to my car to escape the brutal assault. My eyes and face were so bloodied I could hardly see. I made several attempts to run them over with my car, but it proved fruitless as they were easily able to out maneuver my vehicle. To avoid accepting defeat, I smashed my car into her parked vehicles several times before heading to the police station to report the assault. The charges I filed at the police station that night were eventually resolved in court with a slap on the wrist for them both: they were sentenced to a scant probation and community service.

I find no joy in telling this story, but it's worth mentioning because of the many lessons I learned from it. Over twenty-five years and three surgeries later, I maintain diminished hearing in my left ear from that assault—a small price to pay for my life, which could very well have ended that day. However, the story's lessons didn't stop there.

It was a couple of years later before the three of us would ever be face-to-face again. They had come to Savannah where I was living at the time to visit other relatives. My aunt and I used this awkward opportunity to reconcile, and we agreed to forgive each other and mend our fences. However, her boyfriend (by now, her husband) adamantly refused to acknowledge any transgression on his part, or even to forgive me! He forcefully shouted, in much the same rage as when I had last seen him, that he would never forgive me.

Twenty-four hours later after they had driven back home, I received news that seemed like poetic justice. I got a phone call saying that he had been shot and killed in the very same place we'd had our altercation earlier.

The last words I ever heard him say were "I'll never forgive you!" Now, it seems he was absolutely right about that. I'm eternally grateful for these powerful lessons of love, humility, and forgiveness. I only hope that by telling this story these lessons will help enhance the lives of many others. It's unfortunate that they came about through such a tragic experience, but these lessons were for me to learn from and apply to my life; they weren't meant for him.

I n the afternoon one day, when I was living in Fort Lauderdale at age 35, I was laying on the sofa watching my daily religious programs before hurrying to work the 3-to-11 shift just down the road. I watched religiously and would never miss my programs, even if it meant being a few minutes late for work.

This day, however, was different. I was watching an episode about fulfilling your God-given destiny. I lay there on the couch, pondering the words in this message and how it applied to my life. Thinking of my destiny naturally caused me to assess my past as well. It was about 2:30 in the afternoon when I had a sudden epiphany and insisted on knowing why my life had been inherently unfulfilled. Up until now I had operated much like a robot controlled by others. I literally relied on others to chart my destiny.

What to do and who to emulate had always been decided for me by others. For the first time in my life I felt it was safe and reasonable to question God directly without an intercessor.—something I was taught never to do. My inner thirst for knowledge outweighed my fear of damnation and forced me to pose the most difficult question I'd ever asked—because I needed an answer:

"Why do I believe in Jesus?"

Yikes! I hesitantly asked the question out loud with anticipation that a ball of fire might be thrown from the heavens to consume me.

The moment I posed this question out loud, the answers came out loud as well.

"Aaron, you believe in Jesus because you've been taught to believe in Jesus!"

As if the floodgates had been opened, the follow-up questions began flowing:

"Who taught you to believe in God and Jesus?"

"My parents did, of course."

Tears streamed down my face as I released the pent-up anxiety of wanting to know just where I fit into the universe and with God. This avalanche of questions and answers continued as though the answers had been inside me all along, just waiting for this conversation to happen.

"Well, who taught your parents to believe the way they do?"

"Their parents, of course."

Now, this awareness alone was no reason to abandon what I believed, but I thirsted for the truth. I became aware that I might be squandering my divine birthright to know God for myself, on my own terms. Until now, what I had learned about religion and God was on others' terms. Continuing to live my life based on others' teachings could have dire consequences. It even occurred to me that the people who had instructed me on what to believe might have doubts of their own about the religion they followed!

Eventually I dragged myself to work an hour or so late. My heart felt significantly lighter, partly because my epiphany had lasted an hour or more, but also because the Lord had not struck me down, nor had any fire rained down from the heavens. With each passing moment, I felt more and more hopeful that I might live to see another day. My awareness of religion had just undergone a momentous paradigm shift, and I began to perceive that God was within me and that I was within God.

—✳︎—

These questions and answers would continue for several weeks. I was tired of being led around like an animal on a chain. The preachers who I knew personally were eloquent Sunday morning orators, but I knew many who were more concerned with the material world than the spiritual: wondering how much money their members would give them in honor of their tenure anniversaries, and even having extramarital affairs. They were certainly capable of inspiring a crowd to jump to their feet and shout "hallelujah," but did this mean I should trust their message? No longer could I be convinced to believe in something just because the words were uttered in fancy phrasings and parables. I respect that others have a right to their own religious perspectives, but beating me over the head with their perspectives and interpretations only provoked me to find truth elsewhere.

My new awareness invited me to introspect. I found myself meditating on my life, day and night, looking within myself to discover who I really was in my relationship with God. Had I, in fact, become a person who was molded and shaped primarily by the religious influences around me? Could I have possibly lived the first thirty-five years of my life based on instructions that were flat-out wrong? Was I not capable of relying on myself and being a self-thinker? This was the first time in my life that I accepted that I was inherently gay—when I understood that, for thirty-five years, religion and society had attempted to change that against the intentions of the Universe.

As time went on, I became more and more sure that God was on my side. Even if I had said or done something wrong, God's love would forgive me. This love nurtured me through my long odyssey of awakening and awareness. I was learning to sense God as I never had before: as the ultimate source of love. I had always been told that God is love, but now I knew that God's love is beyond our normal definition of love. Human love, by its nature, has boundaries and prejudices. But for the first time in my life, I knew that God's love is *pure* love and nothing else, without preconditions or constraints!

My religious interpreters—my parents, elders, and pastors—
assumed that they were put here to direct my path. It turned out
I had been misled, although their intentions may have been good.
Fortunately, this misdirection did not disconnect me from my Source.
As it turns out, Source was simply waiting for me to acknowledge its
presence and cultivate my own spiritual awareness. No longer could
I be satisfied with the self-contradictory message and the perplexing
hypocrisy of the religion I had embraced wholeheartedly. Convincing
me that God loves me, while deliberately setting my life on a course
of confusion and inner chaos, would now take a lot more than hurling
subjective interpretations of Bible scriptures at me.

PART II
AWARENESS

*Except during the nine months before he draws his
first breath, no man manages his affairs as well as
a tree does.*

George Bernard Shaw

While I was growing up, my mother told me that the stove was hot when the burner was on. It certainly became my belief, based on the sincerity of her admonishment, that if I were to touch that burner, I'd get burned. But it was not until I tested this out when she wasn't in the kitchen that it became my truth, my knowing. Only then did I know for myself that the stove was indeed hot. There is a major difference between believing and knowing when applied to any other aspect of our lives—especially religion.

As a little boy being hurried off to Sunday school every week, I often wondered how heaven could be any better than where I was right then. I was a typical boy—other than my slight speech impediment that caused me to stutter. I had all the fantasies of most children. Christmas to me meant new toys, and Easter meant lots of candy and a brand new Easter suit to wear when I would say my Easter speech at church. Not many kids would want to miss any of that, and I was no exception.

My life was full of enthusiasm, anticipation, and a burning desire to participate in life on my own terms. I anxiously looked forward to the opportunity to grow up and jump into life. If there was, in fact, this meeting in heaven we all had to attend, for now I wanted it to wait!

The enthusiasm inside my most inner core felt like heaven already, if not better, especially since I hadn't had a chance to personally scope this other place out for myself. Like all my Sunday school classmates, I too was sold on the beauty of heaven, described to me by the elders at church. However, that alone was not enough to convince me to give up my life here on earth.

Being told that a new house will bring tremendous joy is not quite the same as owning the home and living in it myself, where you can form your own first-hand knowledge that the house brings me tremendous joy . . . or not. In the same vein, who would purchase a car based solely upon the rhetoric and enthusiasm in the salesperson's delivery pitch? I suspect that most would want to drive the car for themselves to form their own opinion of the vehicle. Yet we would have to admit that, when it comes to religious beliefs, we blindly accept what the church tells us.

It's possible that my parents, along with my Sunday school teacher, the pastor, and the elders in my church, were honestly trying to prepare me for the life they assumed lay ahead. But could it be that they themselves were still grappling with their own spirituality, and took solace in indoctrinating others, with hope that their own doubt would be eroded? I suppose that they might have been unsure, and were merely passing on what had been passed to them.

One thing is for sure: none of them had actually ever visited this place called heaven, though they spoke of it so eloquently. If they had, they could have given me a first-hand account of what was there. Then again, why not let me check heaven out for myself so I would have my own knowing and knowledge of it, just as if test driving a new car I wanted? For it is in that instant of actually driving the car that my beliefs about the car become knowledge. You might convince me to believe some things you tell me about the car, but until I drive it myself, I will not have the *truth* I seek.

This to me represents how religion contradicts spirituality, and it explains how religion has been able to do tremendous harm in separating us from God, our Source. Religion requires us to follow and believe what others tell us, and that is why I do not follow organized religion. On the other hand, seeking to understand our own unique relationship with God, the universe, and our Source—for ourselves—is spirituality.

Religion is the practice of taking our minds and lives and turning them over to others, allowing others to handle information and disburse it to us. If I seek my own awareness and explore my unique connection to the universe, that is spirituality. And that is where I choose to operate.

M y objective in writing this book was to encourage us all, at a minimum, to realistically examine our beliefs—especially how and why those beliefs came about. Government and religion are intent on laying the ground rules for us to live by, and our mob mentality to be like others creates a false sense that society's values are our own.

Government and religion have set the moral expectations for others to live by, and these rules have not always been in the best interest of mankind. Consider this: at one time, only rich whites could vote—blacks and poor whites were not allowed to vote. As time went on, laws were changed so that all white males could vote, yet blacks were not afforded the same right. Next, black men were granted the right to vote, but no women were afforded the same right. Eventually, everyone was granted the right to vote. But still, blacks and whites were prohibited from marrying. Eventually, interracial couples were allowed to marry each other, but only if they were heterosexual. Today, gays can adopt children, but many states still prevent them from marrying. History shows that this too will change.

Our government and religion established each of these turpitudes, and many more. The masses blindly followed, only adjusting their moral compass once religion and the government adjusted theirs. In each instance, love ultimately prevails. This long road had to be traveled only because society had resorted to exclusionary rules and superiority complexes. If love had been the societal rule from the very beginning, none of these morality battles would have ever needed to take place. But even today, these fights for love and acceptance wage on.

Nothing allows us more opportunity to examine how our beliefs are formed than our moral assumptions: what we accept as being right or wrong. Because our minds are where we make these moral determinations of wrong or right, the mind is a great place to start our examination.

Given that man only learned to write some five thousand years ago—and hasn't always told the truth—exactly how our moral assumptions came about remains shrouded in mystery. We were all born into this world without prior knowledge. Subsequently, we had to make sense of all the gibberish we heard, so we learned to put words together in a way that made sense as a language. But somehow, we learned to manipulate that language in a way to impose rules and values upon others.

Whether it's animal cruelty, polygamy, spousal abuse, or child abuse, what is it within each of us that determines the moral stance to take? How was the moral assumption made that we should or should not care about the environment, or protect it for those who come after us? We were all born without knowledge, so every one of our values and morals is learned behavior.

These learned behaviors and beliefs, arbitrary but strong, make us contradict our own natural impulses. We can desire peace, but easily be provoked to fight; we can say that we love, but then justify our hate and hostility. We encourage fidelity and honesty in others, but fornicate and cheat on our taxes.

Imagine a speeding driver who cuts you off in rush hour traffic, and then gives you the finger in rage because you didn't slow down more to let him pass you. Now stop to think for a moment. Do you believe the other driver was morally wrong for doing that? Who set the standard for your determination? Most people would agree that the other driver was in the wrong. But does the fact that most people would agree with you make your viewpoint right? Our interpretations of right and wrong are so deeply ingrained in our egos that there's hardly an objective view to consider.

There are many other instances where we apply our preconceived notions of right or wrong, and it's worthwhile to explore where we may have gotten those notions and how we use them. I, personally, have never smoked, and I'm quite annoyed when others smoke around me without my consent. But let's be fair: what authority established this moral value that one should not smoke around others? Albeit, secondhand smoke has been proven hazardous, but there are countless other hazardous things that are not only legal, but that society has no problem with. Also, what if the smoke being emitted was not harmful, but in fact pleasant and healthy? Would our moral view then change?

When the government makes laws that we should be punished or put to death if we, in turn, killed or harmed someone else, are we to accept the government's interpretation as our own moral belief? Shouldn't we first consider our own innate thoughts on the matter? Religion, as well as government, tend to set laws based on morals that we're expected to abide by, but what gave religion that moral authority to establish how we should behave or what we should accept as wrong or right? If we currently accept religion as our moral authority, we should determine who or what gave it that authority to set those rules for us.

I am not suggesting that one should not aspire to high moral standards, or that one should disregard the rights of others. I am, however, suggesting that we take a serious look at the basis for our moral beliefs and that we determine whether we organically formed those beliefs or if we've been convinced to accept them.

Homosexuality is one of those tests that we can use to assess our beliefs as well. Many people feel that homosexual acts are beyond their moral acceptance, while many others are quite accepting even though they are not gay themselves. A fair question—to those on both sides of the morality aisle—is whether our beliefs are founded on principles established by some authority other than our own.

Who decided that one should not be gay, vote, sit in the front of the bus, drink out of the same water fountain as others, attend the same schools as others, or marry who we choose? When were these rules established, and why do we tend to accept them as our own until the government or our religious leaders tell us differently? Have we not the capacity to determine, within our own minds, what we feel and expect of others? Even more absurd is that we expect others to embrace the same moral values that we've chosen because we think our own moral values are the sole, absolute truth.

When a religious leader in our culture has an affair with the church secretary, while other cultures and religions freely allow multiple sexual relationships or spouses, what morality assumptions— outside of religion—apply? If you reject the religious standard for morality, where will you find that religious morality ends and your innate morality begins? At some point, each of us has to start asking ourselves just who or what handed down these rules that we have unwittingly followed for thousands of years. Did we explicitly grant our government or religion the authority to impose their moral standards upon us, or did others speak for us?

Sadly, others continue to speak for us today; government and religion continue to act as the supreme authority, directing our moral compass. Because of an initial push by People for the Ethical Treatment of Animals (PETA), and the eventual legal backing that our government put in place, an entirely new set of moral assumptions have been established on how to treat animals. The same can be said about laws concerning marriage, abortion, the environment, stem cell research, and so on.

Again, I'm not suggesting that we should avoid responsibility for any of these issues of human or animal rights. I'm merely calling for a thorough examination of why we accept these moral beliefs and why we expect others to espouse a morality just like our own. Our insistence that others feel remorse for stepping on our feet by mistake exudes an egotistical arrogance that we are right, and that anyone whose views are contrary to our own is wrong.

In conclusion, we are a nation of laws and we should acknowledge them, however acknowledging or obeying them does not mean you should necessarily agree with them. It's important to examine all our moral beliefs to see if they are our own, or were handed to us by others. You will probably discover that racism, sexism, and discrimination against others is not an inherent part of who you really are. From here we can begin to see the connection we all share as one with God—and that we have only been brainwashed into believing we are separate from or superior to others.

S everal years ago, I moved into a new apartment. I met the gentleman next door, and over time we became good friends. We'd go to dinner and to movies on regular occasions. We would even meet in other countries when we both happened to be traveling.

One day while having dinner, our conversation turned to religion and the church. He was fascinated with visiting and taking photos of beautiful temples, churches, cathedrals, and sanctuaries. As we chatted about his fascination, he mentioned that he was an atheist.

I was floored when he told me this. I had always assumed he was Christian, and I had never given his religious beliefs a second thought. It would not take me long to reconcile it in my mind, considering what great friends we had become, but this created an avalanche of other thoughts in my mind as well.

I had always been encouraged to have disdain for those who believed any different than I. I was taught that the Jehovah's Witness, Mormon, Pentecostal, and Protestant faiths all had it wrong. We Baptists were the *only* ones who interpreted the Bible correctly. In all fairness, I had to have known that people in other religions felt the same way about their own religion, that we Baptists had it all wrong. But it would have been blasphemous to consider that their viewpoint might be just as valid as ours.

In fact, I had no rebuttal whatsoever for an atheist. It was easy to debate someone of another religion, but how do you debate someone who has no belief or faith to begin with?

Would I now distance myself from the friendship because our religious views were starkly different? No! There was no *rational* basis for me to claim my beliefs were superior, and I understood this. Up until that point, I had not been aware that my religious background discouraged me from accepting others on this level. But why should my friend's beliefs change the way I felt about him? How could I judge my neighbor and friend any more than God would?

The biggest lesson I learned that day was that God created all creatures and all things, and that God loves everyone. This powerful message delivered to me on that day showed that everyone—from nonbelievers to devout followers—is connected by God's love. That is the *true* message of love and acceptance.

It's important to remember that we are all born in a state of natural disorientation, and so we must individually create our own lives from the disarray. For many of us, our choice of religion was made by our parents, who in turn, also had the choice made for them.

We are usually baptized or confirmed in a particular faith long before we even know what faith or religion is. Then, we spend a vast part of our life led blindly by our preacher. We can only hope he or she knows where we are going. And we can only hope that we'll like our destination once we get there.

We listen intently to the lists of dos and don'ts, the shalls and shall nots, that religion puts forth—instructions that we are to abide by for the rest of our lives. However, it is only if we go through self-examination at some point that we can begin to know ourselves—and more importantly, be ourselves—so as to bring authenticity to our own lives.

It makes more sense to me that God would place intrinsic inspiration within each of us—not delegate the task of saving souls to man. After all, man is a mortal being, subject to the selfish whims of our egos.

I distance myself from anyone who claims to be teaching the truth, but is actually excluding groups of people who don't comply with their own ideas of how one should live. I also distance myself from people who are critical or judgmental of those whose perceptions of God are different in any way from their own. Our most natural state is love, and when love is repressed it is most often replaced with hate. We should aspire to reconnect with our most natural inclination, the inclination to love others. We're all part of the same greatness. So if we don't love others, how can we honestly love ourselves?

was married, the father of two wonderful children. Though I loved my wife with every fiber of my being, I also realized that I was married because that's what was expected of me. That expectation had been implanted into me by those in my circle of influence, some of whom perhaps shouldn't have even been married themselves.

For years, I had repressed the hypocrisy of my marriage, even as my attraction to other men lingered. I had tried for many years to wish and pray this magnetism away, but to no avail. This was similar to my growing up, admiring my friends who lived in beautiful homes and neighborhoods, wishing I was white like them. No amount of my wishing would ever make my blackness go away, and likewise, no amount of wishing would make my gayness go away. My masked feelings would come to the forefront when distinguished church overseers and highly-ranked members would proposition me for secret sexual rendezvous. But I never gave in, as my faith and my commitment to my family would always prevail.

For years, I grappled with the hypocritical religious teachings of others. I yearned for a transcendent level of awareness—one that would put my incessant questions to rest. After much soul-searching and deliberation, I requested and was granted a divorce.

—✱—

After I made that decision, which had affected nearly everyone in my life, I was stricken by guilt. I was left to live my life with unanswered questions still. How could I have taken so many years in marriage from someone I loved so dearly? How might her life have played out differently, had I not become intimately involved with her? These were not easy questions to answer, and the only solace I could find was that I ended the charade sooner rather than later.

I spent several months replaying the past over and over in my mind, like a broken record, and I found my emotions all over the map: from anger at those who had hijacked my life, to elation that I now felt closer than ever to God. I had finally moved beyond the self-righteous proponents of fear and transcended the hateful, hypocritical rhetoric of the church. It was then that I started to view the church's supposed message of love as a major distortion of *true* love. I realized that its contaminated form of love had not only affected my life, but also the lives of countless other unsuspecting disciples. Religion had not only weakened my connection with God, but it had also harmed everyone even remotely connected to me.

As it turned out, other areas of my life had suffered under the regime of religion. I had become materialistic, self-centered, and obnoxiously obsessed with greed, envy, and ego. I would constantly compete with others and compare myself to them. I often judged those around me—even my family members—making myself feel good by making them feel bad. My self-worth had been my car, my house, and my bank account's fabricated balance. But now, I insisted on knowing God's beauty and truth for myself. I began to focus acutely on how I might possibly erase my past, or at least find the damn reset button! The day I took on this paradigm shift was the day I surrendered to my Source, thereby summoning God for the first time as co-creator of my life.

—✳—

With very little fanfare, I began to salvage the pieces of my broken universe, almost as if I had been given orders to put my house up for sale. I sold or gave away all the possessions that I had treasured for so long, and I moved to the first city that came to mind: Atlanta. I knew absolutely no one in Atlanta, and that was just the welcome mat I needed to walk across. Family and friends had become my crutches, and I had been using them to hold me up for far too long. If my Source was to become my center, it needed a clean slate to begin with.

When I crossed the state line into Georgia, the burdens I had been carrying for many years were lifted. No longer would those closest to me be obsessed with, or even aware of, my perceived level of achievement. Nor would I compare and compete with their worldly pursuits. I was relinquishing my obsession with my perceived status, and most certainly with the statuses of others. With no more need to be deceptive, manipulative, or pretentious, I became disinterested in the sagas of other people's lives. No longer would I selfishly intimidate the ones I professed to love. Leaving my home was just the catalyst I need to start anew.

My prayer was for God to use my life as inspiration—as a beacon to others so that they would see and feel Source within me. It was important for me not to wear my spirituality on my sleeve, but rather to allow others to sense the power of abundance and the presence of God's love within me. I would have to live my life so that others might be inspired by my actions, not merely by my words. Others who knew me would unequivocally know that if there was hope for me, there was hope for all indeed.

Here I was at thirty-five years of age, and I had lived my entire adult life a repressed, closeted, gay Christian. I had been taught to be anti-gay—essentially, taught to hate myself and had adversely affected the lives of others that were caught in my web of deceit, shame and self-hate. Finally, I could understand that my short-fused temper, my battle with depression, my recent weight gain, and my obsession with material wealth were all caused by my lack of acceptance—by my self-hatred. My being taught to hate gays had taught me to hate myself. But no longer would I hide from who I really was and leave others to direct my destiny.

My incessant demands for more fame, fortune, and recognition ceased immediately, and the ego that had driven me to become financially independent and seek the approval of others subtly faded away. I humbly submitted to my Source and I entered the happiest phase of my adult life. Coming out, for me, meant coming alive—for the very first time in my life!

The decision to tell others that you're gay, bisexual, or transgendered is, of course, a difficult one. And most often, the first question you'll ask yourself before making an announcement is: does my family genuinely love me, or will they act supportive until I tell them I'm gay?

When I made up my mind to share that part of my life—to tell my family and friends that I was gay—I reckoned that if they objected to who I was, I was willing to walk away and never see them or speak to them again. I made peace with the fact that, if my family or friends would desert me or shun me, I would live with that. My resolve was further strengthened when I realized that it would be more of a barometer of their love for me than of my love for them. It was comforting to know that they—not I—were about to face the ultimate test. As for me, I would never again have to wonder whether their love or friendship was genuine, or was merely lip service. Their reactions would determine whether their friendship was worthy for me to have in the first place.

Even if they would disown me, there was very little downside to losing their approval. Ever since I had gotten my divorce and moved away, my relationship with my family had grown distant, and we would hardly talk about my personal life any more. I didn't have the privilege of their approval and blessing, so how could they take it away? Besides, I was already socializing within a welcoming community of friends and peers—without hiding myself.

Like many who came out of the closet long before me, I knew it would no longer matter whether I was the greatest father, had made the highest SAT score, received the teacher of the year award, or won the Nobel Peace Prize. All that would matter to many is that, from that moment on, I would be called "the gay guy," "my gay brother," "the gay Nobel Peace Prize winner,"and so forth. How could every achievement, every accomplishment, be downplayed by one three-letter word? Perhaps I will never understand how such blatant homophobia became an acceptable part of society. After all, we never hear people describe someone as, "that straight guy," or, "my straight brother," "the straight Nobel Peace Prize winner".

I waited for what seemed like an eternity, wondering when the time would be right to tell those closest to me. Finally, I realized that any time is the right time to test the authenticity of love. Let's face it. When I talk with my family or friends on the phone, we always end the conversation with a heartfelt "I love you." Sooner or later, that claim has to be tested.

I'm exceedingly glad to report that my mother and most of my family passed this test of love with grace and honor. To the sanctimonious others who feel compelled to critique, condemn, and criticize: I offer you my love and acceptance anyway.

I assume that it's news to many, because it certainly astonished me when I discovered there were loving, respectful gay communities, very much alive, operating invisibly within the broader community. I'm talking about prosperous, healthy, flourishing communities of gay-friendly venues and businesses. During the time I was married to a woman myself, I hardly knew of the openly-gay venues or the thriving businesses that were right under my nose, and I had never sought to explore them. Perhaps I was even more surprised because I had lived my life in the South, which has been slow to adopt even racial tolerance, let alone gay tolerance. Fortunately, my world travels would allow me to see that the larger world was a much more diverse and welcoming place than I knew.

Reflecting on my own coming out, I encourage the youth, along with those still caught in the struggle of how to possibly come out: acknowledge your inner self first, and then share when the moment is right for you.

I would not pressure anyone to come out to their family and friends until they felt right about it. I had friends encouraging me to be more open, but it was I who decided when it was right for me. But as I look back now, I do wish I had come out sooner rather than later. It certainly would have saved me and those around me a whole lot of needless confusion and angst.

Understand that, if others taunt you or talk about you, you will feel hurt—but this is because their hateful accusations are out of harmony with your loving self, and therefore offer a resistance to the wonderful being of the universe that you truly are. By the same token, this is why you feel good when loving thoughts are directed toward you. Regardless of what your parents may lead you to believe, if you were to die or to walk out of their lives today, they would grieve you and would want to have you back on any terms. Unfortunately, it can sometimes seem as though your parents' egos overshadow the reality of their deep love for you.

These principles can be applied not only to being gay, but also to any other feature of yourself at which others spew vitriol, resisting your most natural state of being. You cannot become a better person by aiming to please others. You must know that you are beautiful, made to be loved and accepted. Understand that you are part of God's perfect order. You are not alone. Those who judge you do so to make themselves appear more acceptable. They try to tear others down and build themselves up because they have yet to accept themselves.

As Dr. Wayne Dyer once said, friends are God's way of apologizing for our families. Embrace a supportive network of friends; share with them; lessen the despair. Know that, beyond a doubt, it does get better. Remember and embrace the love from which you originated, the love that you felt when your life began. For only once you truly love yourself will that love come full-circle: in the form of unequivocal acceptance from others.

However, this is where *I* am in *my* own life. I'm now in a state where I'm at ease with who God has created me to be. I am truly grateful for the abundance created in my life today in the form of love, health, wealth, and true friends. There is nothing I wish to change about who I am, and I don't apologize for being myself. I freely offer my love, even to those who act hateful toward me. Although my journey has seen some turmoil and tears as well, it has been a blissful one indeed. I'm eternally grateful for acknowledging my own intrinsic awareness and the spiritual growth that led to the tranquility I enjoy today.

I'm deeply grateful to my mother for her love and acceptance of me, but there are a frightening number of men and women who are not that fortunate to be born to parents that aspire to the higher ideals of love. As a message to the gay youth who find themselves in the struggle to choose between being hated for who you are or being loved for who you are not—understand that the church or others cannot give away something it does not have whether, love, acceptance, tolerance or even food. There are fortunately many churches and organizations that do offer love and acceptance and will freely share their resources with you.

My family and friends may disagree and often do with my unorthodox views or the manner in which I live out my own life, but they would have to resoundingly agree that I live my life my way. I define success as living your life as if its your last! My freethinking approach—independently seeking enlightenment and thus applying my own reasoning—is totally out of sync with those who insist on conformity.

It's simple: the more you love yourself, the more you love God. The more you love God, the more you love yourself. This connection is certainly no coincidence. My fervent quest to know God ended up with me knowing myself, as well.

I continually nurture my awareness of all abundance in my life today. Simply acknowledging the awareness assures its continuing flow into my life. I have no issue living within my means, as long as I can continue to take the limits off those means. I wholeheartedly expect and anticipate abundance in my life. Publishing a book that inspires and encourages others to accept that the universe is our celestial storehouse in which we can shop twenty-four hours a day—is evidence of my inherent rewards. This awareness has nothing to do with fame or fortune, in which I have little to no interest; I would rather seek the quietness and anonymity I've come to enjoy.

During the time when I conformed to society by being in a marriage, I felt loved, but incomplete at best. I'd often hear from other married couples that their goal was to prolong their marriage at any cost because God commanded that. Rather than to enjoy a quality marriage it was more a demand to be fulfilled. It was as though the one who spent the most time in any marriage—even suffering in a bad marriage—would get a prize at the end! What a colossal waste of their lives and their time to be imprisoned in such an unfulfilling marriage!

"We've been together for seventeen years," they would begin. "The first two or three were great, honey, but the last fifteen have been pure hell!"

"Yes, but I hung in there, darling."

"You fool!" I would usually reply.

Who the hell would stay in a unhappy relationship for so many years and then have the nerve to brag about it? But today, I am acutely aware that so many couples do just that. Sometimes it has to do with their insecurity or codependency, but more often than not, their religious beliefs are the real reason. The religious notion that one should suffer so as to achieve status of some sort is, to say the least, misguided and archaic dogma.

—✳—

With all the hoopla about gay marriage, and since I identify as gay myself, one might assume I'd be a staunch proponent of the marriage equality being debated today, but not so much, and here's why. According to recent census information, the overall number of marriage filings are rapidly declining. Many already contend that marriage as we know it will be obsolete in a few years, or even that it's already obsolete. I do believe that everyone should be equally entitled to commit to whomever we choose, but for different reasons, I'm against marriage—for gays and straights alike.

Before agreeing that you ought to "protect the sanctity of marriage," first ask yourself, "what sanctity?" The institution of marriage in this country has become such a sham: close to half of all the marriages in our country end up in divorce. The only real winners in these cases are the attorneys and the courts, who profit from divorce.

Furthermore, marriage has become more about disenfranchising select groups than celebrating love. Consider that marriage in the United States provides over 1,400 legal benefits[4]: community property, joint tax returns, joint insurance policies, pension plans, medical visitation, inheritance, and more. Consider that when a heterosexual couple lives together but is not married, they don't receive these advantages; but if they choose to marry, the benefits begin immediately. Now, consider that in most states, a homosexual couple still cannot choose to marry. In essence, they are deprived of these rights, which should be inviolable.

The blurred line between church and state has given government the authority to choose who to reward with incentives and who to disenfranchise. I question why the government is involved in marriage at all. Shouldn't it be a matter of the heart? If marriage is a personal, religious, or spiritual concern, why does the government have a say in it in the first place? How could a just government sanction marriages

---

4   This manifold list of benefits was compiled by the Government Accountability
     Office, so as to help determine how marriage equality would impact citizens
     from a legal standpoint.

from only certain religions, or between some couples but not others? Under a just government, any two consenting adults would be granted the certificate of commitment.

Let me share an interesting piece of research done by the Barna Research Group, a Christian organization that aims to understand how Christians believe and behave. Of atheists, 21 percent have been divorced, while 29 percent of Baptists have been divorced and almost 27 percent of Christians overall. Also noted was that conservative Christians got divorced at a higher rate than liberal Christians, and Christians getting divorced at the highest rates were among those most likely to oppose gay marriage or complain about the state of marriage. The highest rate of divorce was found in the Bible belt among the most conservative states.[5]

The research concludes that any threat to marriage in America is, perhaps, the unstable state of marriages of Christian conservatives, not gay relationships or even godless atheists. Those findings are mirrored by other independent research studies as well.

The tradition of marriage, in and of itself, is not flawed at all—it is merely a commitment between two consenting adults. However, the government's involvement in the institution is flawed beyond measure. It was a dramatic eye-opener for me, moving from being married to a wife to being married to a husband. Just by decree of marriage to my wife, all those important legalities were taken care of automatically. But the moment I had a husband, we had to consult with an attorney to protect the very same rights of commitment.

My partner and I had celebrated our love and commitment long before the government sanctioned our marriage. We continue to honor our *personal* vows—not a marriage certificate—and recognize them as the paramount declaration of our commitment to each other. That marriage certificate is simply to serve as a record in the court, as legal evidence of our commitment to each other, and as a token of our support of equality for all.

I truly believe that if churches and policymakers had concentrated on strengthening existing marriages—instead of attacking others— then gay marriage wouldn't have taken such strides so quickly. But as it is, churches concentrate more on disenfranchising gays than on improving those dire divorce numbers, and their strategy of fighting will only ensure that gay marriages become widely accepted within the next few years.

To make this point more clear, look at some of the things that we have chosen to fight, and take a look at the results. The War on Terror has only gotten us more terrorism.[6] The War on Drugs has gotten us more drugs and more drug-related problems. And the war on marriage equality has resulted in more marriage equality. You can even take a look at the Tea Party's war on what they perceive to be socialism. They fight the idea of socialism, but disingenuously, they refuse to relinquish our current social programs. Their fight is misguided at best, and it will most certainly result—you guessed it—in even more social programs.

No one I know of has illustrated this point better than Mother Teresa: "I was once asked why I don't participate in anti-war demonstrations. I said that I will never do that, but as soon as you have a pro-peace rally, I'll be there." She embraces the virtue of a non-warring mentality. Far too often, we overlook the wisdom of the spiritual figures who lead by example, and we focus instead on theatrical, self-centered, and confrontational leaders. Perhaps, instead

---

6   A broad spectrum of security experts and politicians, who tend not to agree on much, do agree that the War on Terror is inefficient and counterproductive; it has increased terrorist recruitment and increased the likelihood of attacks against the US and its allies.

of attacking others, we need to focus on peace. To fortify marriage and return to the tradition of commitment, we must erase our politicized and hate-based definition of marriage, expanding it to a spiritual one that recognizes the commitment of any couple that has true love.

S ince I came out, I've had the enlightening experience of meeting many peers who live their lives in the closet, rather than dealing with the possibility of harsh rejection by their church, family, or friends.

Some of my peers hold very high positions at work. At the company Christmas party, where their coworkers escort significant others, they find it more palatable to show up alone, rather than with their partner of the same sex. That way, they think, no questions are asked.

Of course, this leaves their partner at home alone to deal with the rejection. "How long do we keep up this charade?" they ask themselves. "Why don't we live in a world where we can all be accepted?" The mental anguish continues: "I can't talk with my parents, siblings, or anyone else. My life has to remain a secret to those I love the most!" The incessant torture goes on for years, until something gives—often painfully.

A good many of these closeted individuals attend church religiously. They are often married to someone of the opposite sex, sometimes they even have children. They are doctors, firefighters, engineers, teachers, politicians, preachers, and lawyers; and they excel in their endeavors. They own successful companies and they balance careers and family. Some even preach or teach Sunday school.

But these gay, lesbian, bisexual, and transgendered people fear coming out. Their fear is heightened by the homophobia perpetuated by their church and society, by preachers who demonize gays and lesbians. How can a religious body reject its members, yet expect those same members to espouse the very beliefs that condemn their inherent spirits?

It is dispiriting to see so many loving people holed up within themselves, unable to express the love they feel inside because they fear being ostracized by friends and family—who might really only *profess* to love them. This dreadful fear of persecution outweighs, in their minds, the benefits of being able to freely love the person they choose.

One of the saddest things I see today are gay and lesbian youth who have been ostracized and filled with a fear that God hates them. They've had their minds, souls and spirits hijacked by those no more capable of minding their own lives. They're torn: in one direction by a religion they were given by others, and in another by their inherent sexuality. I have male and female friends who have, against their better judgment, married someone of the opposite sex—just for the sake of pleasing their religion and family. It always proves to be in vain, though, when they are later scorned for being unfaithful or living on the down-low. Witnessing this pain inside others, struggling between what the church taught them to believe and what they inherently feel inside, has been painful—to say the least.

It's important to remember that, one way or another, society always finds a way to criticize—regardless of your sexual orientation. I had the choice of either remaining closeted and being criticized for who I'm not, or coming out and being criticized for who I am. I chose the latter. But where did we go wrong? How did character assassination—sometimes that of people we profess to love—become so routine?

Today I feel an overwhelming sense of validation, a gratefulness to be identified as gay. For if I had not been spurned by the doctrines taught in the church, I may not have been inspired to think for myself, to learn to know God for myself. It's a dreaded thought to have lived my entire existence holed up in shame for no tenable reason. If I had accepted the notion that even though God loves all, it was righteous to deny others our love, I may have never sought to reconcile this clash of doctrines. Of course, as I found out, the discriminatory message of the church is impossible to reconcile with the love inherent to the human soul.

Family and friends alike, it's time for all to get aboard the love train and stop the religious based hating on those you inherently love. It's about love and nothing else. Be who you want to be and allow others to be who they are. There is absolutely no virtue in denying the love and acceptance you envision for yourself to others. You will inspire so much love in the universe by doing so.

've had discussions over and over, with friends and foes alike, comparing African-American civil rights with the current gay rights movement. My stance all along has been that, although there are differences, the two struggles are incredibly similar: it used to be impossible to be accepted as an African American, and now I yearn to be accepted as a gay man. In both issues, we cry to be accepted for who we are—not who others desire us to be.

Some people, on the other hand, make the argument that they feel the issue of gay rights is being shoved down their throats. Others indicate that they can't advocate gay equality because their religion finds it unacceptable. I respectfully disagree.

In my mind, the crusade for equal rights for African Americans is no different from that for equal rights for gays. After all, they're both human rights, and they both affect me directly—I'm a member of both groups. And when I bowed under the pressure of society's expectations, acting straight while feeling gay, it was just as realistic as hoping that society would see me in a white body although I was really in a black one. I cannot do any more about my being born gay than my being born African-American—as I had no role in either.

By the same token, I can wrap my mind around the difficulty that others might have understanding this. If I were a white heterosexual male, I would have no reference to what being black or gay was like; just as I don't know what it's like to be a white woman or an Asian man, either. In fact, if I cannot relate to what it is to be straight, it makes sense that straight people would have no idea what being gay was like, either. Hence, we should drop that half-baked argument.

Even though I don't know what it's like to be someone I am not, I find it a worthy compromise to accept people the way they are, and to accept them in love. It's worth noting that the NAACP has taken a forward-thinking stance on this issue, as well. They opposed Proposition 8 that was to ban gay marriage in California. The organization recently elected Perry Ravi, a 28-year-old openly gay black man as its president for its Worcester chapter, saying, "This is a human rights organization, and we have an obligation to fight discrimination at all levels." Members of different ethnicities have been elected to various positions within the NAACP as well.

The solemn necessity of this acceptance should weigh heavy on our hearts, because until all of creation coexists at the table of togetherness, society as a whole will continue to flounder. Strength cannot be achieved through division; it can only be obtained with unity.

Let me introduce one of the great unsung heroes of the civil rights movement: Bayard Rustin, a black organizer. He had a huge impact on the freedoms we all enjoy today. Rustin was central to the advancement of black equality, and more largely, of human rights worldwide. While other civil rights activists were in the limelight, Rustin was kept in the shadows for one reason only—Rustin was openly gay.

In fact, it was Bayard Rustin who organized the hugely successful *March on Washington for Jobs and Freedom* where Martin Luther King, Jr. delivered his now-famous speech, I Have A Dream, in 1963. Rustin was an advisor to King and together they formed the Southern Christian

Leadership Council (SCLC). Later on, he became active in the protest against the Vietnam War, and became a champion of gay rights.

I strongly recommend watching *Brother Outsider: The Life of Bayard Rustin*, a film about his life and his contributions to twentieth-century America.

In 1987, the year before his death, Bayard Rustin asserted in a speech that *The New Niggers Are Gays:*

> Today, blacks are no longer the litmus paper or the barometer of social change. Blacks are in every segment of society and there are laws that help to protect them from racial discrimination. The new "niggers" are gays. . . . It is in this sense that gay people are the new barometer for social change. . . . The question of social change should be framed with the most vulnerable group in mind: gay people.

This is not to say that black oppression has disappeared. He simply calls upon us to look objectively at how both racism and heterosexism are bred from the same resistance to love and acceptance.

To become more accepting, we should first see ourselves as an extension of the universe that created us all: much like how an apple is an extension of the apple tree. Once we understand that we all originate from the same Source, we'll no longer have the tendency to reject those we thought were so different from us. Despite our differences in race, creed, or sex, we'll know that we all originated from the one divine Source.

—✳—

My earliest memory of prejudice was in the first grade. I was the first in my family to attend a desegregated school, from the first through sixth grades, in my small Florida town of Merritt Island.

My three older sisters had attended a nearby black segregated school until then. One day, I remember raising my hand several times in class to ask my teacher if I could be excused to use the bathroom. She repeatedly denied my request, but she would allow the white kids who asked to be excused. I was mindful of her authority in the classroom, but after awhile I was unable to control my bodily functions. I crapped and peed in my pants. She forced me to sit there in my seat until school was out and I could go home. I did not come to understand until much later that these new laws forced her to have a black in her classroom, and that perhaps her mind wasn't ready to comply with those laws. At the time, I only perceived that she didn't like me; I had no idea why, for I was really fond of her.

Of course, my parents and grandparents endured much more difficult times. Many of our ancestors bled, fought, and died for the right that we take for granted today—the right of being considered equal to everyone else. Although I regret their pain and suffering, I rationalize that the burden was uniquely theirs. It was their time to be alive on earth. Our entire world is a better place because of the pains they endured. Their burden may have even enlightened them in ways we'll never understand.

Even with all the rights and freedoms we enjoy today because of our ancestors' sacrifice, we still tend to focus on the lack in our lives. We sometimes take for granted the battles that were already won. We mustn't do this. If we don't reap the rewards of their sacrifice; their blood, sweat, and tears would be in vain.

That said, we will not find peace in holding onto racial hate of the past, insisting that today's generations of white people are somehow responsible for the transgressions of their ancestors. Most people my age or younger had very little role in the struggle or the outcome. Our lives today are much better than our ancestors'. And as we all—blacks, whites, gays, and straights alike—carry the torch of justice on the next leg of this journey, our world, even a few years from now, will be even more just.

In the past, religion was used to justify slavery and inequality for blacks. But as Martin Luther King, Jr. said, "Injustice anywhere is a threat to justice everywhere." He couldn't be more right. This was self-evident when huge numbers of non-blacks offered their wholehearted support for the civil rights movement—a movement that would hardly appear to affect them. Whites and minorities fought on behalf of blacks, just because they felt it was outright wrong to discriminate. The same is true of the gay rights movement today. Gays and straights alike are standing up and speaking out for equality for all. Just because you might not see how a particular inequality affects you, doesn't excuse you to sit on the sidelines. If we allow injustices to persist with any group, we open the doors for our own unjust treatment.

PART III
A MIND OF MY OWN

Do not go where the path may lead, go instead where
there is no path and leave a trail.

Ralph Waldo Emerson

'Ve always been captivated by the United Negro College Fund's slogan: "A mind is a terrible thing to waste." While they are speaking of an education in the academic sense, I'd like to give this saying a more divine application.

On the day you entered your physical existence here on earth, you were given a most vital gift. By supreme authority it was created exclusively for you.

There were many facets of this gift, including your identity and your free will, as well as your connection to your original Source. Since it was the key to your unique qualities, you would have been well-advised to nurture, revere, exercise, and defend this gift—at all costs. But because part of the gift was your free will, even that decision would be left up to you.

A gift so sacred demands maximum protection, yet every single day many people unwittingly abandon theirs. What is it? I'll bet most people wouldn't guess that their mind is their most precious gift. Yes, your mind is your one unique item that distinguishes you from everyone else. It makes you yourself.

Now, would you consider giving possession of this divine gift, your mind, to anyone who asked? Unfortunately, that is exactly what so many of us have done without even being aware.

My experience with business and marketing has made me acutely aware that companies can have the worst products to sell, but if they have astute, mind-based advertisement campaigns they'll still succeed. I, for one, am not a fan of large discount retailers that use the big-box store concept, but I do applaud these businesses for their success in marketing. With clever marketing, they don't need to actually offer the best products or the lowest prices to be successful. For if consumers merely *believe* that they have the best prices or the better products, then they gain droves of loyal customers who will flock to their aisles without considering any alternatives—often bypassing merchants who can deliver the same or better product for less.

I have many friends and family members who are loyal to just one store—and refuse to even consider shopping anywhere else. Of course, once they're in the store, they'll certainly find the one or two items that they were looking for. And those items might even be on sale. But by the time they make it to checkout, so many extra items have wound up in their basket that they might wonder what happened. The company's objective was met the moment it got you to avoid competitors and come directly to their store instead.

Retailers are not alone here. Politicians, preachers, drug manufacturers, media outlets, and even our own government use these same mind-based marketing techniques for their own gain. In 1984, the Los Angeles Times disclosed how our government dealt with a surplus of cows' milk. They launched an ad campaign that promoted milk consumption, so as to lessen the surplus. All they had to do was blanket our airwaves with TV advertisements and "official government reports" telling us that we needed to drink more milk, that it was healthy and good for us.[7] As you might imagine, milk consumption skyrocketed after the government ad campaign. They were able to put a desire for milk—a supposed need—into our minds. Nearly thirty years after these campaigns started, I know parents who still encourage their children to drink cows' milk, saying, "it's good for you," without actually investigating on their own.

Mind control of this sort goes on every day. As you can see, organizations merely need to get their messages into consumers' minds. Like a well-oiled machine, consumers will follow the company's directives. Only basic maintenance is needed: just keep filling their minds with fresh oil.

We're living under a spell that we seem unable to wake from; meanwhile we follow these companies, preachers, and government agencies in an endless lockstep to nowhere. Why do we remain on this dull and meaningless path of accepting the world as others say it is? Is there some point when we'll quit selling our one utter uniqueness— our minds—to others? In the course of our spiritual awakening, we need to muster the courage to reclaim this invaluable birthright of our minds. Only by regaining control of our minds could we possibly have an open and free mind, so that we may embark upon this journey and reconnect to our Source.

---

7   Some believe that cows' milk is only meant for calves. There have been many studies that show nature did not intend it for human consumption. Moreover, the fact that we drink cows' milk makes us the first and only creature to never wean off of milk after infancy, and in fact, to continue to drink it well into adulthood.

All I have seen teaches me to trust the creator for all I have not seen.

Ralph Waldo Emerson

Every individual—including the preacher—is shaped by his or her thoughts within the infrastructure of their minds. Our mind has a vast resourcefulness within, but most of us have far too narrow a view of our own mind's significance in comparison to the larger universe from which we all originated. It is up to each of us to reclaim our own awareness of the fascination, mystery, magic and awesomeness of God and the universe. We must not become too infatuated and immersed in the symbolic status of names, titles and positions we hold as human beings. To do so would make us more akin to slaves of others who either envy or relish our carnal status and label us accordingly.

We must acknowledge and come to the realization that we are mutually participating in the huge cosmic affairs of the universe where we observe trees, moonlight, clouds, and stars, and not remembering the awe-inspiring magnificence of our relationship to it all. A lack of this perception renders us mindfully ineffectual when we are so much greater than even our own creation, and are ourselves co-creators of the amazing universe. Our minds are more akin to nature than man and therefore, we can not continually look to religion and man to solve our inherent need to be one with nature and God.

Knowing that God is invisible, peaceful, and silent, yet conquers and accomplishes all things without fighting or demonizing others, are crucial lessons about God and nature that we must relearn. Repudiating others goes completely against the omniscient nature of God. Any doctrine that embraces that notion is flawed and self-serving. A religion that teaches truth would not exclude anyone. The limited ability of a religion and the church to access a higher spiritual truth and awareness restricts its ability to render just rewards or punishments. This inequity alone calls into question the need for a more authentic, sustainable, and truthful relationship with God.

We should therefore challenge our religious leaders on beliefs we do not inherently agree with, beliefs that do not resonate within our own hearts to be true. There is profound hope in remembering that we originated from a nature of love. This is not a liberty we should take lightly or trust to others outside our own connectedness with God.

Man's nature of seeking to control the mind of others through religious indoctrination makes any religion susceptible to mind control. The nature part of man is his mind, and not a prize to be won by someone else—but neither should you squander it. Your mind is your birthright intended for you alone to trust, and you should honor that privilege. If we only operate on a level of our human comprehension, we would be blind to all the peculiarities that exist in nature and God. Subsequently, we fabricate falsities to justify our understandings of God and nature of that which we cannot fathom. Religion is then often used to explain the fabricated understanding.

As a result, we have built multimillion-dollar megachurches for the sole purpose of petitioning God on our behalf in the name of religion. We view them as our intermediaries to heaven and God. But God and heaven are not destinations as portrayed, but a state of being that's within each and everyone of us at this very moment. So why the need for an intercessor to petition on our behalf? Our world seems to be no better off with the addition of these middlemen and beautiful megachurches. In fact, an unprecedented number of wars have been waged, battles fought, and countless lives lost in the name of religion. How has religious propagation helped when so many families, marriages, relationships are destroyed in the name of religion? In the end no one emerges victorious. All are defeated or at a loss.

Countries and cultures have been divided by religion for centuries and will continue to be divided into the future until enough people seek to embrace a higher worldview of a connectedness we share with God. Most religions allow no alternative ways of serving or entertaining another viewpoint. In fact, most discourage any exploration of other interpretations. Somewhere along the way we acquired a cult-like belief that God is cut off to us, and therefore we need to rely on the voices of a chosen few to subjectively point the way toward eternity for us.

Some religious intermediaries have become respected and revered for preaching un-acceptance; hate and fear; and estrangement from our creator while in the pulpit. Pastors often lament that we are lost and separated from God, and then emphasize this belief, further distancing us from the extraordinary awesomeness of our supernatural awareness and connection to God. Consequently, this further contributes to the followers' view that the church is the only way to God. Our faith, hope, and future does not lie within an institution, or within the judgment of man.

For the life of me, I cannot fathom a God who sits on some throne, judging and rejecting the very beings it created. Why imagine such a judgmental and critical God watching over us? Which God do we actually serve? The accusatory one, the benevolent one, the incapable one, or the one who is out there watching and waiting for men to pick up where God left off?

When we inherently feel that God is out there somewhere, why do we throw in the towel so quickly to accept the views we're fed? We must embark on our own expedition for truth! Had we not sought further exploration, we would still believe today that the earth was a flat disk of land floating in the ocean.[8]

This is not a privilege we should take lightly or trust to be directed by someone outside our own connectedness with God. Again, you should challenge your religious leaders on beliefs that you do not inherently agree with, beliefs that do not resonate within your heart to be true. Likewise you should weigh in your own heart, even the thoughts I share with you. Your birthright is not a prize to be won by someone else. It's your God-given birthright that you may either squander or cherish as you choose.

---

8   It's worth noting that earlier Bibles perpetuated this unproven belief and made several references to it: "The pillars of the earth are the Lord's, and he hath set the world upon them."(1 Samuel 1:8)

Experience has shown me that you get the most value in a transaction when there's no middleman. May I suggest that, when we become self-thinkers, we've eliminated the middle man that stands between us and the universe? Ponder for a moment: do we truly need a government, a politician, or a preacher telling us that we should love others, even those who are not like us? Aren't we able to use our inner reasoning to make decisions and come to our own conclusions? Yet we consistently defer our reasoning to a prejudiced middle man.

When we follow religion, it creates a gap between us and our source, ensuring that man seeks instructions from the religious order instead of looking within or looking toward God. It dictates what is acceptable and what is unacceptable, professing that obedience to its rules makes one virtuous. Since these religious intermediaries have positioned themselves between mankind and God, they keep mankind detached from a direct relationship with God.

Our propensity for following others, as opposed to leading ourselves, has led society to embrace social injustices as truths. We must become the opposite of conformists: we must become self-thinkers.

—✳—

Henry David Thoreau, Ralph Waldo Emerson, Martin Luther King, Jr., and numerous others were vilified for going against the masses. These spiritual leaders marched to their own drumbeats of conviction, so they discovered morality on their own instead of yielding to society for their values.

At the time, the public chose not to be associated with these free-thinkers. Instead, they sided with government, allowing its abominable laws to dictate beliefs about morality and ethics. Many times, these free-thinkers were jailed or even lost their lives for standing up for their convictions. They were labeled *misfits*, *rebels*, or *troublemakers* . . . but today we revere them as heroes. Most of our schools today teach students how these revolutionaries changed our world for the better and made it what it is today.

A poet and minister, Ralph Waldo Emerson asserted in his essay *Self-Reliance* that it is our minds that make us sacred. He went on to insist that no law can be more sacred than that of our own nature. He understood that divinity was not, in fact, contained within our churches—as many still believe today—but rather within ourselves, in our minds. He understood that it is how we use our minds as a resource to think for ourselves that makes us sacred, not running to the front pew when the church doors swing open.

Martin Luther King, Jr. advocated equal human rights through peace and non-violence at a time when our government had laws on the books promoting human inequality. The law required that black people sit in the back of the bus, attend segregated schools, and use separate restrooms and water fountains. He was a visionary, preaching a message more forward-thinking than even the most radical thoughts of his day. His message was one of universal equality.

And it was far before the Civil War that Henry David Thoreau balked at the atrocity of taking land from Native Americans. It was by following his inner heart and mind that he was able to change the world, although many scorned his beliefs. Quite relevant today are the volumes Thoreau wrote on balancing our inner convictions with the laws of our government, religion, and society.

There are many times when the laws and rules of the world are at odds with our inner convictions. So how, then, do we reconcile these conflicts? I don't suggest that we break these laws. However, we must not allow the rules set by government and religion to dictate our own moral and ethical thinking. We should instead be guided by our own inherent knowledge of good and of God.

These perpetual battles for our minds have been waged for thousands of years. Sometimes, we wait for some authority to tell us what to think on the hot issues of the day, and refuse to think for ourselves. Other times, we disagree with rules but follow them anyway—just to get along with the crowd. And sometimes, we set out to change the status quo by slowly but surely petitioning the government to enact the laws we truly wish to live by.

What are your thoughts on some of today's issues? Abortion? Immigration? Stem cell research? Gay rights? More importantly, how were your beliefs formed?

To truthfully assess your own beliefs, ask whether they're based on your own free thought and free will, or if someone or something else set parameters for what you should believe. If you were *taught* to feel the way you do, you should deeply question your beliefs.

These are serious questions of self-awareness that need to be truthfully answered if we are to rise to our highest calling. For ages, spiritual leaders have called upon man to find their higher selves. Buddha, Jesus, and Patanjali, to name a few, insisted that we not conform, but rather appeal to a higher awareness. Even the Bible taught to "be not conformed to this world: but be ye transformed by the renewing of your mind."[9]

I'll admit that ever since I was a child, there has always been a bit of a rebel in me. Perhaps that's true about all of us. A path of going along to get along never appealed to me. Something inside of me would not conform to those around me. I could not readily accept the American Dream, the conventional lifestyle that others told me I should pursue. I found it intrinsically rewarding to challenge societal norms, and go against them. My rejection of conventional beliefs has oftentimes pitted me against my family and others. But their resistance has only provoked my thirst for further inquiry.

9   Romans 12:2

*The only thing that interferes with my learning is my
education.*

Albert Einstein

In our country of compulsory education, grade schools, colleges,
universities, religious institutions, and our parents are supposedly
responsible for educating us—and for the most part they do a
reasonable job. But what they do not teach us is how to think.

Although we have been born with the most amazing gift of intellect
right between our ears, we are never even taught how to open the box.
In fact, the one common thread among all the education and higher
learning institutions is that they all teach us *what* to think rather than
how to think. It's astonishing that we have so much faith in a regulated
and restrictive system of education.

Our bodies—right down to our cells—are constantly renewing
themselves. The kidneys and heart we have today are not the same
as the organs we were born with, as the cells that make up our
bodies are in a state of constantly renewing. It would make sense,
then, that our minds should be in a continual process of renewal,
as well.

Our gift of reasoning sets us apart from the animal kingdom. Animals usually change to fit their environment. A lizard, for instance, might change its color so as to blend in with its environment. When winter shows up, animals naturally grow a longer coat of fur to adapt to their surroundings. However, we as spiritual beings have been given a wealth of intelligence in our minds. Unlike the animal kingdom that changes to fit their environments, we are able to use our thinking minds to change our surroundings instead.

But just for the record, the last time I looked at a university's course offerings, a class on thinking was not even offered.

I was taught that I should work hard if I wanted to achieve a great deal. I found this plausible, and when I did so, I even found it stimulating. However it did not give me any lasting fulfillment. What if I had instead been taught to try less if I wanted to achieve more—using the power of my mind's thoughts to achieve results? What's frightening is, what if we live our entire existence without ever opening the box that would allow this?

It seems radical to suggest that anyone should not work or strive for achievements of their desires, because there is inherent joy and satisfaction in pursuing our goals and ambitions.

I would suggest, however, that we analyze how closely our thinking mirrors what we've been taught, and challenge our present thought patterns in a realm outside of the perceptual thinking that we've been taught.

We are taught very early in life to recognize and give names to everything in our universe, including their opposites. Hot is opposite of cold and good is opposite of bad. We're taught how to figure math problems; we even host national contests on the accurate spelling of words. Yet we're not taught to think for ourselves.

Far too often we let others dictate what goes into our intellectual treasure when we should instead be exploring and discovering the mind's vast resources of intelligence.

We are taught that creation is great but never that we are greater than creation, and in fact that we are our own creators. Our creation is only a small part of our existence, as it is up to us to then become our own creator through the use of our minds. Einstein is quoted as saying, "You can't solve problems with the same mind that created them." I personally find gratification in this bit of wisdom, and in the deliberate use of my mind as my co-creator.

Schools and universities routinely taught creationism, but after that became too difficult to explain or understand then the teachings focused on evolution, which was much easier to comprehend and accept by many. It doesn't matter which you choose to believe as long as you make the choice.

It is in this vein of unrestricted thinking that we can begin to understand our connection to the universe.

We're taught that we are "here" and the stars in the universe are "out there." We're never to think and question our own perceptions, considering that, from the perspective of the stars, we'd be the ones "out there." The same could be said about heaven and God. Are we really "right here" while God and heaven are "out there? I suggest to you that from the perspective of the universe we and God are everywhere.

Time is a matter of our own perception, as well! For evidence of this, reference the fact that the Ethiopian calendar has thirteen months as opposed to twelve and has a seven-to-eight-year time difference between its calendar and the western calendar. September 2010 was the start of the 2003 Ethiopian year calendar.

This is where our obsession with giving everything names, presenting even intangible things in false dichotomies, needs to stop. In our worldly education, we are taught that the first step to understanding something is to name it and define it. This works fine for things in the physical realm, but when we try to define intangible things in the same way, confusion ensues. Take, for instance, love, heaven, and—most of all—our Source: they are not easily defined in the physical.

You may ask yourself, "What is the opposite of love?" It comes to us without thinking, like a reflex: "Hate, of course." But this is not the case. Love is wholly a oneness and not a duality that can be divided.

When we gave heaven a name, we took it from being a blissful state of being here on earth to an empty promise, like a carrot being dangled just beyond our reach.

Most egregious of all is our bastardization of God, our Source. By giving a name to God, the ultimate unnameable, we moved away from the truth. When we gave God a name, we made God into a person—a very worldly, imperfect person. We even refer to God as "him." We've taken the spiritual and created it in our own image that we might better relate. Tell me: how could the ultimate Source be benevolent one day and vengeful the next? How could Source be anything but constant? But when we fabricated a name for the unnameable, we created a lie.

Source is a oneness and it absolutely cannot be divided. It has no opposite. The moment we try and divide or define our Source, it loses its oneness and becomes a falsehood. If somebody says that "God loves you but . . . ," the moment they add "but," they've created a duality in God which can't exist in a oneness. They are no longer referring to God, but instead to a limited and prejudiced figure.

It is absolutely vital that we not only acknowledge, but also become acutely aware of, the oneness of the universal Source.

Through our education, we are taught to define these paradoxes as a means to understanding them. To recognize that we are here and everything else is out there is purely a matter of assumption that you're standing here—but what if you're standing out there at the time this assumption is made? Out there would become right here. If recognitions are what our teachings are based upon, then that too warrants being aggressively challenged. Intellectually we could reason that if both are here and yet there at the same time, there is nothing to divide us. This shift in our thinking would allow us to then see that we are all in the exact same place at the same time. We and the universe are all either out there together, or right here together, whichever way you choose to see it. This awareness helps us move beyond what we can see, hear, and feel for ourselves, and to acknowledge our connection to the universe.

When we perceive a temperature as hot, we can only do so by comparing "hot" to our belief of what cold is; otherwise we'd perceive temperature as nothing or no-thing. In this analogy our perception of cold and hot becomes one and takes on the oneness in the universe. We only think of others as fat, ugly, or tall because we have been taught to compare with skinny, pretty, or short. During our compulsory schooling, part of the required curriculum was to acknowledge and create these distinctions before graduating to the next grade. You can begin to see how many of the perceived prejudices and judgments about others have come about. If we have learned these behaviors, then in turn, we should be able to unlearn them as well, to again experience the oneness of the universe.

Because we can understand things by comparing them to other things, we accept this belief as factual when we are subjectively determining our truth. This is difficult to grasp for those whose ingrained prejudices of their past are so deeply embedded. Air, rain, sunshine, and blue sky are provided to all equally, with no duality.

Why do churches, professing to be spiritual learning centers, refrain from teaching about the many different religions of the world, to allow a more objective perspective of religion? It would be educational and informative to know about great spiritual teachers who taught and inspired others long before Jesus was on the scene: Lao Tzu,

Confucius, and Buddha, along with the Greek philosophers Socrates, Plato, and Aristotle are just a few. These insightful masters gave wisdom that is as valuable today as it was centuries ago. What role, if any, should these great spiritual leaders and their teachings play in our lives today, not to mention what happens to those souls who came along a century before Christ who were not privy to his particular teachings? It would be commendable if churches fostered an open dialogue to answer these questions in an open forum of dialogue that would allow all to participate in knowing God individually.

Consider these quotes by some of these insightful teachers long before Christ and be aware of how these thoughts still apply to our lives today:

"Learn what you are and be such."

Pindar, Greek poet (522–438 B.C.)

"When the mind is thinking, it is talking to itself."

Plato (428–327 B.C.)

"As a man thinks in his heart, so is he."

Solomon, King of Israel (10th century B.C.)

"Where fear is, happiness is not."

Seneca, Roman philosopher (4 B.C.–65 A.D.)

"The nature of man is always the same; it is their habits that separate them."

Confucius (551–479 B.C.)

"Every man is the architect of his own future."

Sallust, Roman Historian (86–35 B.C.).

Surely there are ways to teach God's universal love, and respect our individuality, that might actually improve the lives of mankind. Realize that the kingdom that many of us desperately seek is, in fact, within the abundant resources of our minds. We therefore do not have to rely solely on outside influences to direct our soul's path. Teaching and encouraging self-actualization to finding the God within each of us would be a major step in that direction.

> *I believe that banking institutions are more dangerous*
> *to our liberties than standing armies.*
>
> *Thomas Jefferson*

I, like many others growing up in America, was sold on the American Dream.

Society tells us to, first and foremost, purchase and put our name on a piece of land. We are encouraged to buy a house early on, preferably in a suburb, with a garage and white picket fence, as well as a shiny new car for the driveway. It's expected that when we marry and have kids, our life will be joyous. We were promised a retirement pension, as long as we stayed loyal to one company in a good industry for thirty or forty years. A quality education and a little hard work will ensure that we attain these things . . . right? And we'd better not falter, for if we fail to meet these milestones, we'll be the misfits of society.

It's amazing how deeply the American Dream has been embedded in our society and in our minds. Even our government rewards those who adopt the Dream with tax breaks and other incentives.

We've become obsessed with living up to the expectations of others, running up the career ladder, buying oversized homes and cars, all the while looking to others for approval to validate our insanity. Unfortunately, it took me amassing an exorbitant number of material accumulations before I realized that the more things I owned, the more those things end up owning me.

Within the mindset of the American Dream, working overtime is not considered a drag, but rather a perk that permits us to buy more things. Never mind that we'll never have time to see or use those things. We work more, buy more, and have bigger and bigger bills coming in the mail. And of course, we have to have insurance to cover the things we accumulate. After all, our greatest fear is of losing everything we have.

On the off chance that we take a vacation to get away from it all, we often cut the break short so we can come back and keep an eye on our things, or so we may return to the work that will allow us to buy more. Meanwhile, it's incredibly stressful to keep up with all these possessions. We've been convinced that it's sane to pay on a property for thirty years while it falls down around us. And as we become impatient and dissatisfied because these things don't really bring the joy the Dream promised us, we take it out on our spouses, family, and friends.

As I look around our home, I see several books and pamphlets on achieving the American Dream. Other books tell us how to be more outgoing, how to get ahead in society, or how to achieve more for ourselves. The world we're raised in encourages us to be extremely goal-oriented. I don't have a problem with that, specifically, but many of us spend too much time striving for goals that *others* have set. When will we focus our efforts on our own dreams?

The books available to us are filled with useful information on how to out-maneuver or out-think the next person for our own selfish gain. Sure, this literature has helped many of us reach this American Dream, but I'm more bothered by what it doesn't teach. Few and far between are books that inspire a deeper existence: one that's individualized and tailored to you. That is precisely the inspiration I'm hoping to awaken in you.

If you ask someone who's already achieved this so-called Dream, you'll probably hear it's not all it's cracked up to be. I've personally achieved these milestones that others set for me, and I can say first-hand: it's not the dream I'd been sold. Having been saddled with mortgage, automobile, and education loans, I was essentially a slave to others—not at all in a place I wanted to be.

We tend to say it's smart to buy a home and car, calling them "assets" despite their constant need for maintenance. We're told that it's a wise investment and that it makes us uniquely American. But haven't you ever heard a homeowner explain how their homes are just a bottomless pit into which they pour money? And given the magnitude of the recent housing crisis, owning all these things has become even more of a nightmare. Adding insult to injury, the meager fourteen days a year of vacation time that our employers grant us must be spent repairing or upgrading our houses. If we don't, they'll collapse on top of us!

More insulting is we've been taught that big banks are our friends and have been encouraged to make them ours. A $350,000 friendly loan could costs us $850,000 or more over thirty years not including the relentless insurance, taxes, and maintenance. When our friendly bank in pursuit of greed recently got in financial trouble, we were told our friend is too big and powerful to fail so we must come to its rescue and bail it out of its misery so it can continue taking advantage of us. When did we become convinced that this entire scenario is a good one?

To me, it's most astonishing of all that the Dream covers our entire period of existence on this earth. Do you really want others dictating what you do for your entire life experience? The government suggests that we retire at age sixty-seven. Retirement would finally allow us to travel freely and take a real vacation. Unfortunately for many of us, our health may not. At least by this point, we should hope to have our mortgage paid off. But insurance, taxes and maintenance never cease. Our "most valuable asset" will sit free and clear of a mortgage, but it will have been in vain. This "asset," for which we've sacrificed our entire life, is nothing more than an expensive shelter. At this age especially, we would find cash and freedom much more useful than this shelter that has ongoing expenses and needs constant repair.

Personally, I was never completely passionate about achieving these goals, but I did find a certain comfort in them. Being handed a set of goals by society was much easier than formulating my own I suppose.

I do not want to discourage anyone from having a life and possessions that brings them joy. I would like to question our motivation for following to a T what some would call a worn-out nightmare rather than a dream. We would be well-advised to separate the dreams that were programmed into our minds from the dreams that are, in fact, our own. Because to many of us, if we were to rationally think about what that Dream proposes, it would seem quite nightmarish indeed. This is our one certain shot at life, and the thought of living it according to the expectations that others have set is harrowing and absurd.

The day I turned eighteen, my mother fulfilled a civic duty in making sure that I fulfilled mine: she took me down to the voter registration office as a birthday surprise. While completing the form, I saw multiple choices for party affiliation. Not being very familiar with politics, I turned with a confused gaze on my face, making eye contact with my mom. She signaled with a nod and quiet whisper of the letter *D* that I should check the box next to *Democrat*.

I'm sure this is nothing new and that it happens all over the political landscape; certainly, it happens in the community where I grew up. I've since changed my political affiliations, several times through the years. The fact, however, remains that I was "born" Democrat. I had no earthly idea what a Democrat was at the time I signed up, but like my religion and other propaganda, I was sold on the belief that I should be a Democrat.

In this same way, I grew up believing in a jolly old fat guy coming down a chimney that we did not even have, only to one day realize it was all a fairy tale. Unfortunately, I have friends and family members who still today will not even consider an alternative political or religious affiliation.

This is not to suggest that Republicans, Democrats, or others should change their party affiliations, but rather to examine their beliefs as to how and why they're associated with any particular party. While each political party has different approaches to achieving its agenda, it's important to know whether we came about our decisions in a mindful, freethinking way. Considering the ideas of both parties are rapidly evolving, I will not be hostage to just one. I think all the parties have some ideas that are closely related to mine, but I do not align myself exclusively with any of the parties, because that would contradict my desire for an independently free-thinking society at large; the parties tend to encourage separatism and a mindset of supremacy.

I'm appalled by systems of government that reward nepotism and the wealthy as prerequisites for party leadership; however, I am more disturbed by the ignorance and willingness of the masses that follow with cult-like enthusiasm those that overtly promote separatism, bigotry, hate, and superiority for certain classes.

The issues in the world today cannot be solved by any one person or by any one party, but I also maintain that these concerns won't begin to be resolved or dealt with effectively until the individuals we hail as leaders embrace a silence within themselves and get to know a oneness with the universe. In the wake of the countless preachers and politicians recently that have vigorously defended anti-gay stances in public and have anti-gay voting records while they live gay lifestyles in private, a course in integrity and honesty should be a prerequisite for both preachers and politicians. Perhaps then we could move beyond the self-serving pettiness of politics and the willful destruction of each other's character on all sides.

I have always been amazed when watching political adversaries being interviewed by the media, because it is fascinating to watch the influential power granted to individuals who have been given a platform on which to perpetuate their messages. Ambivalent souls eagerly tune in to the purported messages whether it is hate, discrimination, or racism seeking an opinion to embrace. It is powerful to possess such a coveted tool of persuasion.

Politicians often become the voice of reason for many others not afforded the same type of platform. People hustle to the television with the unwitting anticipation of being told what to think and how to feel about issues or other people. Consequently, they end up down the street repeating the viewpoint they heard as though it were their own. This is a colossal waste of the human mind, forfeiting the ability to use reasoning and logic to think for oneself, yet it's amusing to watch the power of persuasion in action.

Sarah Palin is an interesting case. She has a quality I find astonishing: she's built a loyal following in very short order. She has criticized the media for its bias, but it is worth noting that the same media propelled her rise from obscurity to something of a political phenomena in the course of a few weeks. Entire political groups have been formed to perpetuate divisive and destructive philosophies using the power of persuasion. Could so many individuals not have known what to think before Sarah Palin arrived on the national stage? Or could these followers have actually been waiting for a savior of sorts to articulate how they feel about others?

I may be disappointed that Palin does not share my political views, but I'm baffled even more that she and her political allies seem to display the complete opposite of love and acceptance. It's hard to believe that she totally disagrees with her opponents on every single issue, that she cannot find even one positive thing to say about her political opponents. Such prejudiced, one-sided rhetoric is simply not credible.

It's easier then ever to be influenced with the inundation of so much irrelevant news. As self-thinkers we have to decide what relevance—if any—to give to the content being put forth by others.

We cannot be tricked into believing that our desire for peace or to not attack an enemy makes us less human, patriotic, or less American.

It makes sense that great spiritual teachers such as Jesus and Buddha never wrote anything down themselves. The task of writing down or reporting the news was usually done by the less distinguished followers of these great thinkers, whom I equate with the news pundits of today. It's possible that Buddha and Jesus would have known that the information would have been misconstrued and reported with a bias they never intended, and we can see how that has played out with all the different religions that were born out of the same teaching.

During the Obama campaign, the media did a magnificent job of inciting fear over the Bradley effect, or belief that whites would not turn out to vote for an African American president. That obviously turned out to be hype put forth by the media that did not play out as some had hoped. In fairness to both sides of the political spectrum, Obama and the Democrats I supported won the election, but at what cost to the perpetuation of free thinking that I most embrace? An overwhelming number of voters turned out to cast their ballots; however at issue is whether they voted as they were told, or took the higher road and voted their conscience.

While I have no loyalty to any political party or figure, I'm a huge fan of Barack Obama. I found myself engrossed with the Obama campaign from the start. I worked diligently on his behalf during his presidential campaign, traveling the country extensively. I would fly all over the country attending events, almost as if I were his paid staff. I felt like I was a part of the history I felt certain would be made.

On the campaign trail, I was beginning to see the world outside of the mundane, everyday existences, and understood and respected a larger, more imminent force in play. During TV interviews, when I was asked whether I thought Barack would win the election, I would consistently say that I felt it was his time to be president, and that others would attempt but be unable to derail his campaign, no matter how hard they tried. Even when the polling and the prospects looked dim, I just knew, in my heart, that he just *had* to win the election.

I was so enamored of the authenticity he displayed, I had to remind myself that he's a just politician, and is therefore limited in what he can get done without the support of others. Even more so, he is limited by the scope of his own reasoning and ability to judge.

—✳—

Of course, history played out and Obama won the election by a wide margin. His victory offered encouragement at a time when many of us were feeling disillusioned. After living through several fatiguing years in which it seems backward-facing policies were driven through the Congress, many Americans had lost faith that the government desired to right many wrongs. The once-bright beacon of hope had gone dim, and the aspirations of many were limited to mediocrity.

But now that Obama is elected, I sense a renewed sense of optimism and pride in our world—especially among African Americans. It's clear that Obama has found his calling, inspiring a nation to rise up to its higher ideals, moving the race issue front and center in our country, and revealing a higher self that so many appealed to and embraced within themselves.

As a result of Obama's election, many now feel that they can and will achieve their greatest aspirations. My hopes and dreams were bolstered as well, evident in my writing this book. This is something that will never be reflected in a poll or debated by the pundits, but for many of us, it is just as real as the sunshine that lights the sky.

I don't mean to imply that others across the spectrum weren't motivated by this historical election. Obama never would have been elected if he hadn't had broad support across racial lines. In fact, over three-quarters of the total voters in the 2008 election were white![10] Blacks were forced to acknowledge this fact: the majority of whites are not prejudiced against them because of their race, and are just as open-minded as they themselves are.

I would be remiss not to mention all the whites who not only voted for Obama, but dropped what they were doing in their lives to take part in the election campaign. I met and spoke with many around the country—who treated me with their tremendous hospitality. Many had never been part of any political campaign before and have not been part of one since. This is astounding and is probably under-reported in the news. Sarah Palin was getting all the media attention and could have been misconstrued by some as the overall female representation of white women, which she was not.

Different groups may find Obama's presidency to be relevant in different ways, but I've heard many stories from minorities who were inspired by Obama to begin a deeper reckoning within themselves, to rediscover their pride, and revive their drive to achieve their dreams. I've also spoken with many whites who longed for and were elated to see this day of harmonization as well.

Regardless of how history rates his presidency, this rapprochement will have a profound effect on the resiliency of the human spirit, forever.

During the campaign, Michelle Obama expressed this same renewed sense of pride: "for the first time in my adult lifetime, I'm really proud of my country." However, she was ridiculed and labeled unpatriotic for saying what many others felt as well. Nothing could be further from the truth.

Since Obama has come onto the national stage, Republicans, Tea Partiers, and even a few ill-intent racist groups started to push the envelope on how far they could go in disparaging him. Some said he couldn't have been born on American soil; some said he was a closeted Muslim; some even called him a terrorist! It should be clear that no matter Obama's values, no matter his campaign promises, and no matter if he aligns with their views, minor groups of people will just hate him no matter what.

Now, in full disclosure, Clinton, Bush and other presidents endured a fair amount of criticism of their own. But when *they* were criticized, it was usually because of their views and policies. When

Obama entered the national scene, he was victim of the most blindly hateful personal attacks. We shouldn't kid ourselves. Weren't a lot of these personal attacks on Obama, in fact, thinly veiled racism? But these are of a minority and we should not be sidetracked or convinced that this racism is epidemic, as his election suggested, the majority of citizens in this country are fair-minded.

If we could rid ourselves of the tendency to label and categorize each other, we could in one fell swoop eradicate sexism, racism, and discrimination. In the interim, it's up to us to acknowledge our own spiritual uniqueness, and with acute awareness rescind and not take ownership of labels and criticism hurled at us by others.

The separating of facts from fiction is usually at the discretion and interpretation of each individual, and perceived racism can be attributed to the conceptual-mind's tendency to label others and fit into sub categories those who are not perceived exactly as we are. It is truly a wonderful thing to truly love yourself for who you are and not who others want you to be and not own labels that others place on you.

I'm a black, gay, independent, father, and grandfather who couldn't possibly be more proud or happy being anything else, and I've accepted and love who I am dearly. I suggest those who tote around their label guns for others do the same, because it only accents how unhappy and unfulfilled they are with themselves.

Considering that Obama will be and has been subjected to vile, vicious ridicule and scornful attacks, he has made a heavy sacrifice. Fostering hope in the citizens of our country and our world, while he and his family are scrutinized by their antagonists and the public, is an unimaginably immense sacrifice to make.

Unfortunately others are often envious when you are living your dream or have defined your own destiny. This is true in politics and everywhere else. I've even found this to be true among my own family and friends. It's easier for some to pull others down to their level as opposed to their rising up to their own aspirations.

Although his victory comes at an enormous cost to the Obama family's freedom, I trust that the Obama administration won't get caught up in these trivial, rhetorical battles. When we shift to a higher level of awareness, we will no longer feel defeat when our combatants deride us: their vitriol confirms that we are living life to the fullest, something they have not achieved themselves. Remember, Jesus and many of the greatest spiritual leaders met tremendous opposition— despite their messages of love and acceptance they delivered. But they also changed the world immeasurably with their consistent message of love.

Meanwhile, Obama is inclined to change an institution of government that has been engraved with hate, revenge, and power for decades, since long before he or many of us were even born. I do not look forward to a reelection campaign season full of malicious rhetoric now that he has decided to run for a second term. But either way, we have to accept that no matter how much Obama is criticized by pundits, politicians, and the public, this president's purpose goes beyond politics and has renewed the dignity, hope, and courage of many.

E go can be defined, among other ways, as an overly high opinion of one's self-importance. I prefer the frequently used E.G.O.: Edging God Out, because that's the nature of ego. Our ego is our one single trait that causes our separation from Source, and it's a favorite subject of mine for discussion. If we analyzed what our lives would be like if there were no ego in play, we would undeniably know God as our creator. If we examine our ego's role in our lives, we'll see that ego is purely our self-serving intentions, and that the faintest hint of ego serves to Edge God Out and move us away from our Source.

Some may argue that ego seems justifiable in the earthly realm of striving to accomplish or achieve materialistic goals. However, I reject the notion that an egotistical spirit can be good inspiration when the mere presence of ego moves us away from God. Source is the observer that notices without judgment or prejudice, gets without asking, conquers without endeavoring, doesn't speak and yet gets answered, all without ever asking for recognition.

Each topic and each chapter in this book is directly related to those three words that make up E.G.O. If we could somehow do away with ego entirely, then God and love would immediately be revealed and exalted. There no longer would be a need to defend, defeat, compete, or compare ourselves to others. In stark contrast to ego is Source, which without any selfish intent is beating our hearts, maintaining the planets' alignment without seeking any praise or acknowledgement.

If you're driving a BMW because you think it's prestigious, but a Ford Fiesta would suffice, ego is in play. When we live in a certain home or neighborhood because it represents our status or achievements, then that is ego as well. When we choose a school for our children because of the bragging rights that come with it, then that too is ego. Any time that self is entered into the equation, whether self-importance, self-centeredness, or self-serving, then ego is in action. Our ego does not allow us to cheerfully live in a less pretentious neighborhood, or drive a less eye-catching car that would better fit our budget.

Even attending PTA meetings in order to be viewed as an engaged or concerned parent, or becoming a Boy Scout leader or Sunday school teacher to seek admiration from others could be considered selfish. If decisions to do something are made for any reason other than a completely unselfish motivation, then we are exhibiting egotistical behavior. This defining of ego is not to discourage us from having the desires of our heart but to make us aware of its presence and practice not embracing it.

I know those whose ego is so hell-bent on vigorously fighting to win every conflict they sense in their lives, that their bitter arrogance saturates their entire personalities. The thought of conceding and losing the upper hand is far too shameful or disgraceful to bear in comparison to the serenity and tranquility of letting disagreements go. They emphatically boast as though a zest for wining is a badge of honor to be envied by others.

It is ridiculous to hear adult men complaining of their wives as being the reason that they are not as successful as they'd like, and saying that somehow their lives would have been better had they chosen a better wife. When chatting over lunch or in a corner at a party we listen as they tell all of the reasons they aren't happy in the marriage. But ego causes them to stay and fight constantly with their spouse rather than appeal to the love they have for each other. We all know people who are in miserable relationships, but choose to remain married anyway—for financial stability, fear of being alone, or concern about losing their married status in society. It is one thing if love is the motivation, but more often than not, it's their selfish egos that is preventing the marriage from working to begin with.

We all know the personality type that lives most of life in the rear-view mirror by constantly living in the past, always dwelling on grievances and regrets as their most current inventory. They find themselves tied up in civil disputes, divorce, or even child-support court for an exhausting amount of time, rather than conceding that another person might be right. Ego prompts their eagerness to engage in a demonstration or counter demonstration for every perceived adversary or foe.

I've often seen in families, mine included, cases where bickering and anger is focused on those who appear to have or enjoy more material success or who seem to be better off. The family bickering often results in punishing others by withholding communication, in some cases not speaking for several years. Grudges held for thirty or forty years are not unheard of and lead to the erosion of family relationships for decades. Usually the impasse begins as subtle disagreements but festers into hate and hostilities when neither side seems willing to relinquish their ego. Some seem perfectly content to take their anger to the grave if need be as long as they don't have to appear yielding or as a weakling while alive.

I've had numerous conversations with friends who've had close family members die, and the family falls apart for decades while fighting over funeral arrangements that were made and the handling of their loved one's estate. Once the play for power begins, the lead antagonist turns some against the others. For some, their resolve is so faint that they are left at the mercy of the antagonist to tell them what to think or feel about the other person—even though they've had little or no interaction with the other person, they are instructed to hate and be angry with them. The power play becomes a matter of who can control the most members on the family board and get more unwitting human pawns on his or her side.

Unfortunately, the rules in the rebellion entail little more than the most egocentric self-centered player picking off the weakest-minded players. In short order the revolt has begun, and the passive people are used as pawns for the king to intimidate. If and when the king grants his backing if the other side relents, it becomes okay again for the dutiful pawns to move out and be social with the other side again. This is the egotistical demonstration of love and acceptance by some, while at a great expense to the others.

Because of a self-centered ego, children are cut off from grandparents they've never met, fathers from daughters they hardly knew, mothers estranged from sons they gave birth to, and siblings from one another. That is the reality of EGO: Edging God Out.

The tyrannical rampage destroys every salvageable remnant of virtue, intimacy, honor, and respect in exchange for the egotistical satisfaction of defeating others. This combatant and antagonistic personality leaves scant room for a truce or treaty with those who rebuff or confront their egos. When we allow our egos to wish harm and despair for others, the lapse in our judgment is made apparent. The notion that somehow there is less available for us, because someone else has received something that we desire, has to be banished. For one thing, this ideology acknowledges lack of abundance by implying there is less for me because you have taken too much. In addition, the notion that someone else being worse off will somehow make you better off is absurd and enforces the belief that tearing down someone else will by make you better off by default.

There is usually a vast difference between the way we view ourselves and the way that others view us. Seemingly no allowance is given for others to grow in wisdom, mature from past behavior, or expand their lives spiritually. If we sense we've made improvement in our morals, ethics, or principles but others choose to only remember that we were arrogant, vile or obnoxious—we may have to wear the former banner with them for years and possibly forever. Malicious attacks on our character are usually intended to hurt or break our spirit, but we must continue to align ourselves with God and love.

Once we become aware that someone else's ego is in play, it's pertinent to summon our own inner peace in order to circumvent his or her ego from infringing on us.

Along the way the idea became acceptable to be considered Christ-like while still harboring anger and hostilities for years on end with another. God becomes no longer needed to guide, because ego takes over to defend that role. Frequently these are professed Christians who opt not to speak or associate with each other. My policy and advice has been not to accept the anger of others just because it is offered to me. You are the one in control of your own life. Harboring hate and resentment gives others free room and board in your mind. You do not have to take every gift that is offered, and it's advisable to not always do so. If you do choose to accept other people's gift of anger, hate, or hostilities, it ultimately will lead to more anger and hate and continued retaliation.

We originated from love, and the love is still and always will be here. Let's rethink our watered-down definition of *love*. Others may not be able to give love, because they must first love themselves. If a person truly loves him—or herself then it is impossible not to love others, because the act of not loving means not loving the part of oneself that connects to others. Once we truly begin to experience the love of God in ourselves—and not the made-up version we're accustomed to—we can understand that it's not really us that others don't love, but parts of themselves they don't love.

It is a colossal waste of energy to blame others or try to force them to love us, when in reality, our attempt to do so keeps our own ego in play. In order to get love it's no secret that we have to be loving and give love. If we shift our thoughts more in line with our Source and absent our ego, we can see that God loves us even with our perceived shortcomings and imperfections. We can then see and love others the same as ourselves with all of their imperfections. If we don't put unrealistic expectations of love on others they can't be used as weapons against us either. We should explicitly let go of our egos—and instead demonstrate the love to others that God so freely has given to all of us.

A s I sat today and observed the things within my view, I could not help being aware of the invisible field of energy that connects us all.

This invisible Source grows the grass that I walk upon. It beats in my own heart and in that of the lady crossing the street afar. It beats in the hearts of squirrels who race about to grab fallen nuts from the oak tree that stands effortlessly in the foreground. It too clearly submits to this awesome Source. Yet at the same time this Source suspends the clouds in the sky, rotates the earth on it axis, while simultaneously creating the oxygen I breathe. This Source, this language of love, does not speak, but instead listens.

It is not discriminating, looking for reason to provide for some, and disavow others. It is not searching for differences in each of us but rather embracing all and freely providing the air, sunshine, and undivided love to all in its path. Sensing this awareness is the beginning of knowing and feeling God. This is our chance to rediscover God who we once knew so intimately.

At some point, we forfeited the knowing we had during our nine months in our mother's womb—and even before. At some point we took over from Source, as if we decided we could do a better job at navigating our lives. We must regain this awareness and trusting of the Source that created us. If we look at life in this manner, the problems in our lives today that we perceive as insurmountable will most certainly shrink.

Source has created the most amazing piece of machinery ever imagined, and it's right in front of us: our bodies. Our physical manifestations have enough intricacies and complexities to make the Hubble Telescope look like a toy we would buy at the five and dime store. Our brain alone handles 400 billions bits of information per second. All of the precise inter-workings that have to take place for us to move our big toe alone would blow your mind. Ten million bits per second is received through our eyes alone; then there's the skin, the ears, the nose, and the taste buds! Million bits of information are discarded, and we are only aware of small portion of this information. Take, for instance, the intricate parts that make up an eye: the pupil, retina, iris, and cornea. All these parts (and more) coordinate with the brain, thereby allowing us to blink, create tears, and look in another direction—and all of this happens with no conscious input on our part.

I don't have to stop while writing this book to reset my lungs, heart, eyes, liver, or any of the other miracles of my physical body to continue writing—they are all happening, totally submitted to Source, just as they were when I was being created. Our physical bodies can go to the brink of unconsciousness each night totally submitting to Source for eight hours of sleep and ready to begin another day. This all happens without our conscious control.

Take a moment to ponder why would Source put so much of its God ability and all its amazement and miraculous qualities inside our minds and bodies, but in contrast put the answers or keys for maintaining our connection to Source on the outside of our minds and bodies—requiring that we seek the opinion of the clergy, the president, or the neighbor for instruction? It seems within this intricate phenomena of our mind is a much more likely place.

It's far-fetched to suggest that the key for living an inspired life is on the outside of our minds and bodies when all of these miracles are inside our minds and bodies. I suggest to you that we don't need a Sunday school teacher, preacher, or a politician to devise the path to a God-inspired life. The challenge becomes to accept that you are in Source and Source is in you. If you cannot see God everywhere, in everyone and everything including you, then you can't see God anywhere or at all.

Earlier I talked about my obsession with becoming a millionaire or achieving financial freedom by the age of forty. During that time, I spent a lot of time working and wishing, getting very little sleep. I acted as though I had control of the universe when I would assume control of situations. I had never considered slowing my hurried pace as I tried to attain my self-centered goal, or allowing the universe to work on my behalf, because I honestly felt I was in control. My distorted view of the world at that time directly conflicted with the realities of the universe.

I'd read every motivational or positive-thinking book or article I could get my hands on. Although I found them motivational, the problem was that I had adopted a mindset that the answer would always come from the outside—that I'd get my answers when I got my millions. All the things I was looking for were loosely based on material acquisitions and monetary achievements, and at that point I was not aware that allowing the forces of the universe to assist in my ultimate desires for joy and fulfillment would get me there. The moment I relinquished the control I thought I possessed, the dormant forces in the universe were activated on my behalf and began delivering my desires in the most unimaginable ways.

Never again have I doubted the magnificence of allowing the universe to increasingly expand its abundance at its own pace.

When we allow our Source to unfold in its own time, our existence is able to be lived, loved, and enjoyed in the utter blissfulness the universe intended. More frequently, we spend entirely too much time and energy trying to force things to happen on a timetable we've set based on our egotistical desire to control the outcome—and this is counterproductive.

By practicing slowing the pace, and aspiring to live more patiently and humbly, I've accepted the fact that lasting change cannot be forced. I acknowledge that the Source of the universe does things in its own time. In this same way, the Source governs the four seasons. Fall comes before winter, and summer after spring. We are powerless to rush or change the seasonal order. The universal Source provides that every bird has food available to eat, and mandates that each animal has a thicker coat of fur in the winter and a lesser coat in the summer, no matter which hemisphere they occupy.

All of this awareness in the universe happens with absolutely no input from any of us. Trees and plants bloom and fade to the tune of nature's Source, and there is no requirement or need for us to rush any of these things. This cosmic creation of Source's invisible and mystical energy field that takes care of nature also takes care of us. We only need to allow the magnificence of this supernatural force to proceed at its own intended pace.

Reflecting on my own bliss and the significance of spiritual solutions I've discovered, the awareness is immense. I have accepted that all things into and out of my life have been orchestrated to enlighten my awareness of home. My awareness that neither I nor anyone else arrived here by accident deepens this connection. I made my way into existence long before this physical manifestation of what I see today as a body. That place of origination will always be considered my home, no matter where I am in this mystical universe. Today, as my soul sought awareness of my origination, I wrote a poem on my reflection:

Death is not my home, since that's not where I'm from

Death is not my home, since that's not where I'm from
But neither have I been—this cryptic cloak I'm in.
Now I am distracted. Although I don't know why,

I have eyes that see most everything, but cannot see all things.
I have ears with which to hear all, yet I miss so much.
I'm able to touch most everything but I cannot feel so many things.
I'm able to smell a rose but I cannot smell my fear.
With all those limitations, it's impossible I be from here.

Now that I know for certain that I'm not really here, I can enjoy this time more blissfully, in this new atmosphere.
No reason here to criticize, no time to waste on hate,
Since any given moment now, I'll go home in haste.
All the more reason now, to slow my hurried pace.
So I'll make it home and realize: Wow! That was a beautiful place.

'`ve had wanderlust for as long as I can remember, and I always knew that I would travel the world one day. I wanted to travel, not just for the pleasure of exploring, but for the awareness it would give me of the vastness of the universe. I often dream about seeing places I'm not sure even exist. I inherently feel connected to the entire world. I have a tremendous appreciation for the trees, mountains, stars, rivers, clouds and animals throughout nature.

This innate burning inside of me knew that the world was mine to explore. Not just parts of it, but every place on earth was for me to delight in till my heart's content. I often found myself imploring my siblings and others to aspire for the same: "If God did not want me to see the other parts of the world, then why did he put them there? I do not intend on being born, living, and dying in the same ten square miles!"

I'm sure they must have been annoyed by my insistence and strong-willed nature to share my view of the world. They often might disparage my views, calling them ridiculous, but I never viewed their criticism as an obstacle. Rather, it was a stepping stone upon which to build.

When I would come to set foot on six of the seven continents before age forty, I was delighted. I'm now aware that my love and zest for life and the universe was never merely lip service, and has blissfully led me down a path of inherent bliss, happiness, and joyful fulfillment. It remains painful to watch those who start out the gate of life full of love, hope, and childlike ambition, yet succumb to the bitter despair of self-defeating beliefs that those things are just reserved for others to enjoy. That mindset is unequivocally contrary to the universal birthright granted to all.

My own name given to me at birth, *Aaron*, means enlightened, exalted, mountain of strength, elated, and blissful. I can't help but notice that *elated* and *blissful* have been the words I've most used to describe myself over the past several years. My first awareness of this utter blissfulness in my life began when I took notice of the connection between the energy of being grateful and thankful for all in the universe. I'm convinced that ungratefulness—not acknowledging our thankfulness for what we already have—keeps us from realizing the full potential in knowing God. I liken this virtue of gratefulness as a spendable spiritual currency, redeemable to attract what it is we *do* want in our lives.

It is your innate birthright to enjoy your own individually profound experiences, and I strongly object to those who believe that we should all strive for sameness in our human experience. Far too often, we put up resistance to the wellbeing granted each of us by our birthright. We fail to honor the worth of our birthright when we unwittingly allow others to dictate the terms of our existence. When I submitted my deep appreciation to the universe, indescribable joy and blissfulness were returned to me.

I'm eternally grateful that this part of my personality was nurtured by my mother as a young boy. Her emphasis on being appreciative—giving thanks for everything that came my way—had a lasting impact upon me. I've told her many times of how the things that she talked to me about had a more lasting effect on my life than the things that she disciplined me for. I trust my emphasis subsequently has the same added value in lessons I've passed on to others including my children and grandchildren.

—✳—

Is the city where you live now, the home where you live now, the place you would choose if you could live anywhere at all?

Do you have the partner or spouse you would choose if you could have any partner you wanted?

Are you working in the job or profession you would love most to be working?

If we answer "no" to these questions, it shows that we are not in complete alignment with our Source and bliss. We must expect the best from the universe, and only then will it come. It is at this level— this state of expecting abundance—that we should operate. And we can only activate the Source of abundance if we are able to genuinely show gratitude for the abundance that we *already* have in our lives. This law of abundance cannot be bypassed.

I've found that that by giving thanks and being grateful for all that shows up in my life, it's guaranteed that further abundance will continue to manifest in my life. A positive attitude of gratitude and thankfulness summons abundance, and gives me the assurance that— even if I don't see it now—it's certainly on its way, and it will eventually show up.

Experiencing the loving emotions that come about with sharing our love and gratitude with others is our innate birthright.

—✳—

One day, I was startled by a neighbor trudging up the driveway, just as I was sweeping it off. She had apparently just discovered I had given some dishes to another neighbor, because she began furiously criticizing me.

"Why do you constantly give things away?" she exclaimed!

Of course, she'd never taken issue in the past when I would give things to her.

I was dumbstruck. After reckoning her statements for a moment, I replied that she was right—I do seem to give everything away. "However," I said, "look at what I still have left." I concluded to her that if you can give away so much and still have so much left, then there must be something very powerful about the adage that it's better to give than to receive.

Then it was she who was dumbstruck. The angry look on her face turned to one of humiliation when she realized how silly it was to be caught up in thoughts of lack instead of abundance. Her reluctance to refute me was proof that she realized—if she cared to participate in the cosmic affairs of the universe—she would be best served to start embracing the same.

It is impossible to give and not inherently receive at the same time. Notwithstanding the joy associated with a physical act of giving and receiving something, such as in a exchanging of gifts—the emotions related to the act awakens inner awareness of appreciation for the giver as well as the receiver.

We submitted to Source from our conception to birth with a knowing that we will be provided for. Never once did we worry about where our next meal would come from, or fret that our parents might not take care of us. Then, somewhere along the way, we forgot this submissive state of being and the blissfulness that came along with it. Through our learned behaviors after our birth we built up a resistance to our natural state of allowing and being. It now is our purpose to remember this blissful state once again.

Our management of the resources we already have (or our mismanagement thereof) is a measure of our gratefulness to the universe, as well. How could I be asked to manage a thousand dollars when I had so poorly handled the hundred dollars I was given beforehand? I would in effect be restraining my own access to God's abundance to do this.

Several spiritual teachers spoke of being good stewards of the resources that we already have, in order to access more resources of the universe. These were lessons I learned the hard way. It was only after I began, in earnest, to appreciate what I already had received, that I was able to continue receiving more of the universe's abundance and bliss.

I had been estranged from my mother for the better part of three years, mostly because I was unwilling to forgive her for what I thought were her shortcomings as a mother.

I felt that my father had abandoned me—he suddenly died when I was ten—and now he wasn't around to help me cope with the emotions I had raging inside.

Right after my father's funeral service, my mother called me into their bedroom as she sorrowfully sorted through his remaining things. She sobbed uncontrollably as she told me that my dad was gone now, and that I must now step in and take his place as the man in the family.

Now I know that it was part of her grieving process, and that she was suffering immensely inside. But at ten years of age, I was compelled to stop her hurting, and to help her in any way—even if that meant taking on the impossible role of being the man in the family. Because I was the oldest boy, it seemed to make sense that I'd assume this role.

I would stay busy helping my mom at her auto body shop while my friends were running track and playing football. I felt I was playing daddy while my friends at school were playing at each other's houses.

I spent the next several years wishing I was old enough to get a real job—so I could help my mother out. In the meantime, I would take on odd jobs, like cutting the grass for neighbors or washing their cars, and I would give the proceeds to my mother.

I could not wait to apply for jobs on the day I turned fourteen; I thought I could substantially help my mom raise our family. I had already begged Mr. Saunders, the manager at the nearby Publix supermarket for a job several times, but he always told me I was too young and had to be at least fourteen. My relentless pursuit would not end, and every day after school, I would make a beeline to the Publix supermarket in hopes that he would hire me.

About three weeks later after seeing my determination to work, or fatigued from my constant badgering, he asked me why I wanted to work so badly. In between my tears and gleeful anticipation that he might offer me a job, I sobbed and told him "I really need to make some money to help my mother pay our bills." On that note, he reached into his pants pocket while patting me on the shoulders and pulled out a ten dollar bill. He handed it to me and asked me to go next door to the Eagle Army Navy store, buy two white shirts and a black tie, and come on back to start work as a bag boy. I was elated to help my mom out, and of course she was grateful for my assistance.

Nevertheless, I ran away from home several months later because I felt overwhelmed with being forced to grow up faster than I really would have liked. I resented watching my friends go play soccer after school while I went to work. My dad was no longer alive for me to blame so I harbored deep resentment against my mother instead for putting the tremendous burden on me to take my father's place. I became adamant that my mom should beg my forgiveness for what I saw as all her wrongs, but she never knew or suspected anything was eating me up inside.

By the time I was thirty-five, and my siblings had long-since started their own lives as adults, I was still carrying the burden of being the father that none of us had. I had been especially protective of my two younger brothers, trying desperately to be a great male role model, and never discussed with them that I was gay. But there was no one to look after *me*. By now I knew and accepted the fact I was gay, but the thought of shattering the masculine image I upheld—especially for my brothers—was more than I could bring myself to do. To further compound my inner turmoil, I now had a son and daughter of my own.

I cannot count the many times I slipped out to my father's graveyard, undetected, sobbing like a baby, pleading for my father to please come back. I wanted, if nothing else, instructions on coping with what I perceived was a mean and vengeful world that surrounded me. All of life's uncertainties and my sexual confusion seem more than I could bear. I remember begging and wanting to trade places with him for no other reason than the instant relief I believed it would have provided from the inner turmoil.

My mother was the only living target I could blame and lash out at, and I furiously welcomed every opportunity to do so! It infuriated me that she was unwilling or unable to intuitively sense my deep pain.

The agony I caused by disowning her was that which only a mother could easily forgive. Eventually, the favor was repaid to me when my own children faulted me for not being the perfect parent myself. But my inherent love for my kids, along with this lesson I had learned, allowed me to summon their forgiveness.

I'm tremendously grateful that Mom and I enjoy a most amazing and loving relationship today. The odyssey that led to the love and forgiveness between us began with my own forgiveness and love for myself. Now we communicate regularly via phone and email, see each other several times each year, and take short vacations together when her health is up to it. I listen in awe as she freely discusses her life and past with me. I honor the sacrifices she made to steadfastly provide for our family after being widowed at what otherwise would have been a very untroubled time in her life.

I now understand her conviction to work several odd jobs to make sure we would have a roof over our heads and bread on our table. I praise her courage in handling this burden she didn't deserve. I now see her tremendous sacrifice in putting her youthful heart and dreams aside for the sake of those she truly loved.

I thank her for giving me my heart's only desire on my fourteenth birthday: a fishing reel and rod. It was a major sacrifice for her to do so, but it was one of the greatest joys of my childhood. To her it may have been a small token of love. But for me, it sparked a profound awareness of abundance in the universe, that I could truly have what my heart desired.

Whatever her motivations may have been, she avoided close companionship and she never remarried. As I hear her laughter, I look into her eyes and see that her young, vibrant spirit remains, despite her wizened body.

It's this same spirit of love that compels me to give back to her. I eventually learned that I cannot give away love I don't first have for myself. Just as surely as I can't give away a car or money I don't have, I cannot give away love or forgiveness I don't have. I discovered I must therefore forgive and love myself first for my own pain, and only then can I give any love or forgiveness away.

The powers of attraction state that you attract into your life that what you think about. I had always been fascinated with construction, and I eventually found myself at the helm of a successful company in a position that not only gave me joy, but also financial independence. Concentrating my thoughts on my desired outcome was instrumental in achieving my goals.

When I reached this stage, I found myself at a turning point that perplexed me. I had attained several desires and financial goals that I never would have dreamed possible even one year earlier. I wondered where to concentrate my desires at this point, and I found that the one thing I was seeking more than any other was balance in my life. This word, *balance*, sulked in my spirit for several weeks as I pondered its meaning in my life. I craved to have a life balanced between work, family, friends, the universe, and myself. Everything I had ever desired and allowed had manifested, so I was confident that I could create the balance I craved.

Spontaneously, I made the decision to visit Cape Town, South Africa for a couple weeks. After getting settled into a quaint bed and breakfast at the base of Table Mountain, I rested up in preparation for a wine tour the next morning. For our lunch break, we stopped at a pier restaurant. I chatted with many locals as usual when I travel, but one guy I met would have a lasting impression on my entire life.

It turns out the first friend I made in Cape Town was Walter Bradlcy, a local psychologist. After educating me a lot about life in Cape Town, he invited me to see his office where he practiced psychology. He showed me how much the South African culture value the treatment of the whole person through many holistic health practices, and he encouraged me to open my mind to some of these concepts. I soon found myself immersed in yoga, massages, and other holistic treatment therapies. By Walter introducing me to other locals and showing me many sites of Cape Town, we quickly became like old friends and conversed about everything from yoga and psychology to the laws of the universe.

The attraction between us was surreal. It seemed we had been destined to meet. He would say how it was so wonderful to meet such a soul as mine, and I would reply that he was placed here by God to meet me. On the evening before my flight out, we were having dinner, and the conversation turned to my flying back to Atlanta the next morning. I insisted on taking a taxi to not inconvenience him, but he insisted on driving me to the airport as a farewell show of hospitality. After he slapped both his hands on the table in protest, I reluctantly conceded.

We arrived at the airport, and I checked in while Walter waited nearby. After I got my boarding pass, we hugged and bid our farewells, then he handed me a bag with two wrapped gifts inside. He asked me not to open them until I got on the airplane.

This next part is still a blur to me, but I will never forget the impact it had—and has had on my life every day since. This was post-September 11, and security had tightened at all the airports. I had just been given three wrapped packages just outside the security gates, but was able to tote them right through heightened security without even a question or stare. I felt I had transcended time and space with all the energy and enthusiasm I was feeling, and was stunned by Walter's spontaneous act of kindness. I sat in amazement on the plane trying to absorb what had happened over the last two weeks. I had never mentioned to Walter my quest for balance during any of our conversations, but I felt an overwhelming balance in my spirit as never before. Whatever transpired over the last two weeks, I knew I was not the same person going back to Atlanta that left there a couple weeks ago.

As I had promised, I waited until the plane was airborne to open the gifts. Anyway, I needed the time before that point to reflect and to compose myself. The first gift I opened was a book by Dr. Wayne Dyer, and in big bold print was the title: *Being in Balance*! How could Walter have possibly known that my quest for balance had spurred this trip? Let me suggest that the universe is always at work to match our realities to our desires, and can never fail in doing so. The tears welled up in my eyes as I read the subtitle: *Nine Principles for Creating Habits to Match Your Desires*.

The second gift was a handwritten card that read:

> *Meeting you, Aaron, has been one of the most wonderful experiences in my life. My life and the world has forever been changed for the better because of you.*
>
> *Walter*

By the time I opened the third and final gift, a twelve-month calendar with daily inspirations from Dr. Wayne Dyer, my tears were flowing uncontrollably. This epiphany lasted until we landed in Johannesburg to complete the first leg of the flight. I was already experiencing this new awareness in my life. I felt that my life as I knew it would never be the same, as there was no way after such a profound epiphany that I would remain the same. My entire idea of who I thought I was had evaporated into thin air. Friends had often described me as a free spirit, but my life until that point had always been a bit messy, in the sense that I seemed to always be searching for my place in the universe. Consequently, I immediately started to attract a never-before-felt peace and balance into my life.

Actually experiencing balance in my life was worlds apart from just nurturing the idea of what balance would feel like if I ever found it. I found myself meditating day and night on this newfound freedom and elation. It was refreshing and exhilarating; I felt a calm throughout my mind, body, and inner spirit.

Without outward effort, I found myself distancing from relationships in my life that conflicted with my higher, universal goals. This was done in love, and no hurt was intended toward anyone; it just happened. I was not even aware of the transformation until I looked back in retrospect.

For the first time, I felt that I truly deserved all the wonderful things in my life. I no longer felt the need to justify them to anyone. Great things now had become an expectation in my life, and I could no longer consider them happenstance. I began to notice the serendipitous nature in my life at this point with a keen awareness that my Source was working around the clock radiating love, peace, and abundance into my life.

*Abundance is not something we acquire, it is something
we tune into.*

Wayne Dyer

My "letting go to let God" was starting to return huge dividends in all areas of my life. I had already walked away from the complicated teachings of conditional love in the church. I thirsted for an authentic affirmation and had grown frustrated with what I perceived as hypocrisy within the church and its teachings of division. The love I felt in my heart was in direct contrast with that which religion had provided, and I inherently knew there was a much larger force in play in both my life and the universe. When I loosened the shackles of religion, it felt as though the weight of the world had been lifted off my back.

Although abundance was constantly being created and manifested in my life, I discovered that the more material things I accumulated, the less desire I felt to have them. I found that the greatest joy was in sharing them with others. But this was a difficult balancing act, as this would often distract others from their own connection with Source.

This is a difficult concept to grasp when you don't have much wealth. After all, that's usually when you value wealth the most. It's when you've amassed a bit of wealth that you recognize all the other things in your life that have infinitely more value.

One of the invaluable joys in my life today is having my mother witness and share in the remarkable changes in my life.

During a time, when my mother had driven up to visit me in Atlanta, I got up early one morning to see her outside walking around my herb garden, admiring the flowers and herbs I had planted out on the back side of the house. I asked if she would like to take a ride into town with me to run some errands and do some shopping. She eagerly agreed for the opportunity to spend some one-on-one time with me, as I had been pretty busy with several work projects and had made very little social time lately.

We got in my truck and drove down to the auto dealership where I routinely did business at the time. Knowing my mom's fascination with trucks, I asked her to kill some time by taking a look at all the shiny new trucks out in front of the showroom while I tended to some business on the inside. She willingly obliged, and a short time later I emerged from the building to join her on the lot, where she was admiring a particular truck that had caught her eye. With childlike fascination, she started to ramble off a list of options, accessories, and all the beautiful things she liked about this particular truck.

"Do you really like this truck best—of all the trucks here on the lot?" I asked.

She nodded in the affirmative.

"If so, I want to buy it for you right now—if you don't object!"

Her eyes immediately lit up with overwhelming appreciation and gratitude.

Afterwards, we went inside to complete the paperwork for her new truck, and I wandered outside only to be stopped by a salesman who euphorically expressed to me the magnitude of the act of kindness he had just witnessed. He expressed how wonderful it would be if he could do the same for his mom. It was his heartfelt, sincere admiration that caused me to take note of this manifestation of abundance that had taken place in my life. The salesman, who was just an observer of this act of kindness, was simultaneously inspired and flabbergasted.

After finishing the paperwork, Mom and I left the car lot in her new truck. In her usual gracious manner, she kept on saying *thank you*. I received her thanks and gently remarked that I was only the observer—that God provided the deed. Here I was, letting go and letting God, and it was as if the flood gates of abundance had been opened in every aspect of my life.

This was a very humbling experience for me, as just a short while before then, I mostly knew how only to just get by. Having my roots in a family of overly aggressive and competitive achievers left me lacking the patience and humility needed to immediately master the art of living in balance and humbly accepting the abundance into my life. The balancing act between humbleness and abundance has been a most difficult practice to master, and admittedly, I'm still learning today.

PART IV
RELIGIOUS RHETORIC

You can safely assume that you've created God in your
own image when it turns out that God hates all the
same people you do.

Anne Lamott

Look at some churches today and you'll see that their original message of love, forgiveness, peace, and acceptance has been negated by their new message of conditional hate. It would take scholars more qualified than I to explain how the church today is even remotely related to the original Christian foundations of love, acceptance, and universal tolerance.

Entire ministries have evolved to satisfy an egotistical urge—that of finding others to categorize, hate, and shun. The preachers of these ministries purport to be the mouthpieces of God, spreading lies, claiming that God hates certain groups of people. They enact self-serving rules and perpetuate false dogmas that support their intolerance.

When a beautifully written book like the Bible is used to promote fear, hate, dread, and doom, one can easily forget that its chief message is love, and is in fact its greatest commandment. Whenever we suppress this authentic love for each other, hate is left to take its place.

Perhaps the fact that we're bombarded by these negative messages is why so many of us find it easy and even acceptable to embrace hate. In fact, we find it almost unfathomable to love, unless there are a million conditions attached to that love. The emotions of hate, fear, dread, and doom seem to come so naturally, but we have to make an effort to love and accept ourselves and others. As children, we are inundated with these messages of hate, and they have become a part of our conditioning. Now as adults, we must make a huge effort to overcome the customary hate and relearn to feel love most naturally.

The church today tells us that in order to be pro-life, we must oppose abortion. But if we celebrate life by becoming one with God, is that not pro-life? The church tells us that, not only must we adopt an exclusionary definition of marriage, but we must also be anti-gay. But this is deceptive and fallacious; neither of these views is pro-marriage. Working to strengthen existing marriages would be a pro-marriage stance—and this the church has neglected to do.

It's perplexing that the church has taken divisive positions like these. Nevertheless, the list of hypocrisies and falsehoods purported by preachers and politicians alike goes on and on, each sharing one common thread: hate.

If you are sitting around the dinner table, talking with your family about the distaste you feel for a category of people, then you are a part of the problem—not the solution. If you utter vile insults with your kids in earshot, you are rearing your children to be intolerant of others. More importantly, they will not be tolerant of themselves.

We've seen all the recent attention given to bullying, specifically, bullying of gay teenagers. The news media took on the topic after a college freshman threw himself off a bridge because of anti-gay bullying. In the same month[11], four other American students took their lives because they were taunted about their sexuality. Fortunately there are groups that are helping to prevent this catastrophic loss of life,

---

11   September 2010

like the Trevor Project, a leading organization for suicide prevention efforts among gay, lesbian, bisexual and transgendered youths.

Bullying was once considered an unavoidable part of growing up, but now in fact, it's fueled by our concept of "justified hate." By the time our kids are teenagers, they've already been taught to have superiority or inferiority complexes. If we don't raise our children to believe that other people are inferior, they won't grow up to be bullies. If we sit back and do nothing, allowing our kids' hateful behavior to continue, who's to say that your own child won't become a victim of this childlike but sometimes fatal behavior?

Although there's no silver bullet to make your child immune from bullies, it's been shown that bully victims who have supportive families also have higher self-esteem, and are better able to cope with bullying. So even if you yourself harbor discriminatory notions—that people of a certain ethnicity are inferior, that homosexuality is immoral, or that those in other socioeconomic classes are wretched—you must not pass those notions on to your children. After all, what if it's your child who drives another student to suicide, or who perhaps is driven to his or her own death?

Even if in your case, this conditional hate is not fatal, it still has lasting consequences. Take your children, for instance, who may be grappling with their own sexual identity. It's important to remember that even heterosexuals struggle to understand their own sexual identity. The physical and emotional changes we go through as teenagers are hard enough as it is; trying to reconcile the teachings of hate with one's innate truths often proves impossible. Your message has to be one of unconditional love, unconditionally. The short-term satisfaction you may receive when you paint others as inferior will certainly be negated by the shame that your loved ones will feel as a result.

—✳—

Church leaders, educators, and other authority figures need to be vigilant about lessening the stigma of being gay. But the first line of defense begins within our own homes—at the dinner table. The vicious cycle of intolerance is a fast track to nowhere. The supposedly righteous individual is not led any closer to their realization of God, and neither is the supposed sinner. If your church has shaped your views and encouraged you to rebuke others who are not like you, then it would be wise counsel to examine how your innate views might possibly depart from the views put forth by others.

If you condemn gays, you are reinforcing the stigma of being gay, and that makes it even more difficult for your family to ever have a truthful discussion about sexuality.

Denigrating homosexuality doesn't turn others into heterosexuals. Parents have just as much control over their children's sexual orientation as children have over their parents'—none. If you think you are solving a problem by loudly repudiating gays in the presence of someone you suspect is living in the closet, you are sadly mistaken about human nature. Quite the opposite: if you condemn gays, you perpetuate the closeted, down-low lifestyle—maybe even that of your own spouse. It may be a hard pill to swallow, but that is exactly what you are doing by disallowing an open forum of discussion in your home. It doesn't take a Harvard degree to realize that, if the message that oozes out your pores is that of intolerance and nonacceptance, you cannot reasonably expect your loved ones to participate in truthful conversations with you, whether or not they're in a category that you find so intolerable.

I was encouraged to hear that a major conservative Christian organization, Exodus International, had recently stopped sponsoring an annual event called "the day of truth." The event encouraged school students to "counter the promotion of homosexual behavior," and the organization decided to stop its sponsorship because the event is far too divisive, too focused on hate.

The press release said, "all the recent attention to bullying helped us realize that we need to equip kids to live out Biblical tolerance and grace while treating their neighbors as they'd like to be treated, whether they agree with them or not." Although the organization still espouses the position that gays are not worthy of acceptance, the cancellation of their sponsorship is a step in the right direction: that of acceptance, inclusiveness, togetherness, and self-forgiveness.

After two thousand years of Christianity, the only thing we seem to have become better at is destroying and hating each other. More recently the anti-Muslim hate rhetoric has been added to the list.

With all the hateful rhetoric surrounding us, some have become immune to the messages of hate. They have discovered that acceptance from God comes naturally, even though a judgmental group of religious zealots would argue otherwise. The universal power of our Source does not exist to question our worthiness. To state otherwise would call into question God's own omnipotence.

Just because we might not understand the nature of every man does not mean every man is not entitled to acceptance. In the same vein, our lack of comprehension of how God is able to operate does not make God unable to do so. Our universe is full of love all around us, but the kindness and wonderful deeds of the many go unnoticed in the sea of hate perpetuated by the few. Therefore we must constantly remind ourselves that God's all-encompassing love is the sole solution.

Adopt the pace of nature: her secret is patience.
Ralph Waldo Emerson

The church can build fancy cathedrals only because it has the resources to do so. In the same way, it is only able to give away hate and nonacceptance if it owns those things to begin with.

But just because a church offers you these platitudes is no reason to accept them. In the words of Buddha, "If someone offers you a gift, and you do not take it, then it remains theirs." You do not have to take ownership of the church's hate. This is a powerful concept message in not accepting the hate, anger, and religious intolerance others may offer you. It is, in fact, our decision whether to take possession of the hate and intolerance that is offered to us. We can—and we should—choose to let hate remain with those who offer it, and return to them love instead.

On the contrary, if your church, bishop, or religion offers love, acceptance, and tolerance, then there you will find an abundance of love that they will instinctively share with you.

Jesus, en-route to Jerusalem, passed through a Samaritan village. The Samaritans were not welcoming of Jesus, so two of his disciples suggested that their village should be destroyed. Jesus reprimanded those disciples and showed no hate toward the Samaritans. Instead, he lovingly extended a hand of friendship to them even though they were not tolerant of him.[12]

The reality is that we can never be one with God and nature without wholly accepting others deemed different from us; thus, our objective has to be establishing a direct relationship with God.

How disgraceful it would be for a tree to reject its branches or for a stream to disown its banks; yet we seem to have programmed our DNA to reject anything that is not exactly like us. Only in the human species, through the teachings of organized religion, do we see such widespread rejection—a total opposite to everything in nature and the universe.

Take a moment to ponder: it took two people to make you. It took four grandparents to make both of your parents, and eight great-grandparents to make your grandparents. These numbers grow exponentially. If we look back just a bit further, simple math will show us that, just in the past five hundred years, you had well over a hundred thousand ancestors! That number doesn't even include all of your distant aunts and uncles, or all of your cousins.

Now, take a moment to ponder. Do you know all your cousins? Not just those in your immediate family, but also those connected to you through a distant great-great-great-grandparent? You'll have to admit that you don't. You couldn't possibly know every one of your cousins—because over six billion of your cousins are alive today.

We are all connected, and the math holds true whether we want to accept it or not. This awareness alone should cause us to think twice about the way we treat everyone around us.

---

12   Luke 9:51-56

Although invisible to the naked eye, there are connections between each of us. We cannot see electricity either, yet it still flows. Just because we don't see the connections doesn't mean they're not there. You and I are indisputably connected with everyone else on earth.

We should forget the notion that we are superior and others are inferior in any way. There is a lot more in common between us than there is that separates us. We are part in parcel of the same divine order of the universe and uniquely rely on each other for the sustainability of humanity. We must remember our sameness and oneness and not wallow in our perceived differences. Stars do not condemn the night, and the rain tolerates the lightning. This is the nature of the universe and God

Science investigates; religion interprets. Science gives man knowledge which is power, religion gives man wisdom which is control.

Martin Luther King, Jr.

Growing up in the South, I was taught that we Christians were a peculiar people, meaning that we were different from non-Christians.

But as I chat with the Christians I meet around the world, I realize something. Morally and ethically, there appears to be no authentic distinction between my Christian and non-Christian friends. We all have drinks at the same happy hour bars, we dance at the same nightclubs, and we watch the same R-rated movies.

We all take part in the same pleasures of the secular world. I don't object to Christians—or anyone else for that matter—enjoying the things they find joyful, but these behaviors seem no different than those of any non-Christian.

There is one possible explanation for how some 85 percent of the U.S. population can be Christians: one can become a member simply by saying "I'm Christian." Of course, there are rules that go along with membership, but members aren't expected to actually abide by them.

There was a recent Pew Research study that showed that atheists and agnostics knew more about Christian beliefs then Christians themselves knew.[13] The research goes on to say that evangelical whites were the most knowledgeable of their religion, and Black Protestants and Latino Catholics finished at the bottom in their own religious knowledge. It went on to say that Mormons, who are not considered Christians by fundamentalists, showed greater knowledge of the Bible than even evangelical Christians.

The study seems to suggest several things, including that Christians know very little about their own faith and even less about other religions. It showed a reluctance among Christians to learn about their faith and a willingness to accept their faith as true. They already accept their faith as true and they feel no need to examine it—or the faiths of others.

Certainly, this observation does not apply to all Christians. Many really do earnestly work to live their lives by the principles of love and acceptance that Jesus espoused. However, there are still those who seem to look directly at the world for their cues on how to live a Christian life . . . and their lives become indistinguishable from the lives of non-Christians. They adopt the same ethics and morals that any secular person would.

Christians and non-Christians alike stand before the same preachers for marriage and judges for divorce. And we all tend to worship material objects of our desire, at times. Christians live in as much fear, worry, and frustration as everyone else, despite professing that one should have peace. Their fear leads them to obsess over securing their doors, windows, and bank accounts. Their anxious dread of death is the same as everyone else's, if not even worse. How could a soul possibly find comfort in such hypocrisy?

---

13   Agnostic and athiestic respondents scored at the top of the study, which asked a variety of questions on religious knowledge. U.S. Religious Knowledge Survey, September 2010

*To be free is not merely to cast off one's chains, but to
live in a way that respects and enhances the freedom
of others.*

Nelson Mandela

O ne thing that seems distinctive among churchgoers is their willingness to publicly oppose what they choose to do in private. The parishioners pretend to believe and accept things that they really don't, just so they can maintain membership in the church.

Christians say that their top priority is God, yet in practice, parishioners and preachers alike value possessions, power, or prominence.

Multiple marriages, repeated divorces, and having out-of-wedlock children are considered morally wrong, and yet they're tolerated. Birth control is considered wrong, which most married couples in the church use in some form or another. The church preaches against the very actions that most of its clergy and members partake in.

Some members, because of personal experience, might be privately accepting of abortion or of anything else, perhaps because they have friends or family who participate. But because their acceptance is not in-line with the church's stance, they find themselves having to abhor

publicly what they accept in private. They are deprived of their right
to love of their own accord.

It'd be easier to consider the judgmental a bit less hypocritical if
they quickly rushed to condemn everyone who broke the covenants
they put forth as God's laws: those who overeat, have extra-marital
affairs, excessively adorn themselves with jewelry, cohabit with others,
have children out of wedlock, masturbate, use birth control, or cheat
on their taxes. The hypocrisy is that all these people are routinely
tolerated, but certain Christians, like those who are openly gay or have
had an abortion, are shunned.

We are each unique beings, and we do have to resist adhering
to the expectations society sets. We must identify, within our own
minds, that which is right for us. It is not an easy task being constantly
torn between what is being thrust into our minds and what one's
spirit knows inherently. But it was these ambiguous, contradictory,
self-serving messages of hypocrisy that eventually led me and many
others to seek a more congruous truth above reproach.

The church seems to grant its membership a hypocrisy pass:
permission to practice what the church preaches only during
discussion and debate. The church has no obvious issue with these
double standards, almost as if it expects pastors and church members
to break its rules. The standard church etiquette applies: just keep your
indiscretions under wraps and you'll avoid derision from the church.

Meanwhile, some get emotionally scarred for life when they
believe that others are doing right by the group, making the same
sacrifices that they struggle to execute. The danger in this acceptable
pattern of hypocritical behavior is that it has perpetuated itself for so
long that it is now perceived as the rule rather than exception.

Preaching the moral absolutes of religion and practicing those absolutes have not been one in the same. Not to mention that following those absolutes are difficult or impossible for mortal man. In many cases, they are made for the sole purpose of bragging rights: "I don't do this; I don't do that." We *are* human, after all.

I don't claim that my moral compass is infallible, but this hypocrisy is flat-out wrong. I, for one, think that the moral expectations are far too unrealistic: from the preacher to those in the pews. And I can emphatically state that these contradictory messages hastened the departure of many from the church.

Scandals have torn church after church apart with esteemed deacons, preachers, or Bible teachers engaging in extramarital affairs within the social confines of the church's society, or with clergy sexually abusing children.

The church seems to have taken an "eyes wide open, but I'm blindfolded" stance toward extramarital relationships, out-of-wedlock children, unrestrained fornication, and birth control. The church tends to accept this hypocrisy as a way of life, sweeping the innumerable indiscretions under the carpet. It rebukes only the most absurd social transgressions that have become public. It's as if the church body is absolved of its own wrongdoings when it shows contempt for the wrongdoings of others.

I'm convinced today that if all the members who were gay, adulterers, molesters, fornicators, hypocrites, and thieves were to leave the church, then the church would be devoid of its entire congregation. Even the preacher would have to walk out the door!

At what point does the smoke screen disappear, allowing our real beliefs and actions to show? How is it that one can get so comfortable living in hypocrisy? With ease, the religious seem to find contentment in living a life opposite to the standards they have for others. They are often the ones who say that they love, but in fact harbor hate and hostility. They pretend to have peace while their lives are full of anxiety.

Every now and then, the veil *is* lifted, revealing scandalous and blatant hypocrisy. Entire lives are turned upside down. Adulterous relationships are discovered to have existed for many years; out-of-wedlock children are acknowledged; homosexual relationships are uncovered. These are just a few of the devastating experiences that unsuspecting victims are left to deal with. And when the sufferer turns to the church for support, to reconcile this occurrence dispensed by a God who is said to love them unconditionally, the only consolation they provide is that the burden is solely theirs to bear.

Our complacency and acceptance of these hypocritical stances as the status quo is what has to change. We can begin by making a silent dedication to execute our lives in a way that pleases us and God—and not one that is necessarily pleasing to the expectations set by others.

America will never be destroyed from the outside. If
we falter and lose our freedoms, it will be because we
destroyed ourselves.

Abraham Lincoln

Many churches today have become more like political institutions than religious ones. Some have become so involved in politics that, in many cases, more time in the pulpit is spent on secular politics than on spiritual matters! This leaves their followers baffled as to whether their role is of a parishioner or of a political advocate.

Church leaders are waging battles outside the church that they have not yet won *inside* the church. Intolerant parishioners, taught to hate, are sent out to defend a doctrine that they themselves believe only half-heartedly—so they hardly do so enthusiastically. They protest on street corners against abortion rights, gay marriage, and stem cell research when these issues have not even been resolved within the church body. As you can imagine, I find it more than a little disturbing when Christians attend rallies to change the world from the outside, without first changing within themselves. Really, this has been the *true* spiritual abortion of the church.

The church has already lost many of the political battles that it started. This once-invincible institution is akin to a wounded animal, staggering about, licking its own wounds. These mounting political losses call into question the long-term viability of the church.

Even James Dobson, "the nation's most influential evangelical leader,"[14] concedes that these battles are lost:

> We are awash in evil and the battle is still to be waged.
> We are right now in the most discouraging period of
> that long conflict. Humanly speaking, we can say we
> have lost all those battles.

The church's approach, destroying others in an attempt to build itself up, is flawed to begin with. This only leads to more fighting, but ultimately, love will conquer hate. This is evident throughout our history: just look at the fights against civil rights and women's rights, and the current fights against abortion and even gay rights. Progress has been made on all these fronts even though they were met with a fierce oppositional force. These historical accounts confirm that there is no virtue in hate. Anger has only served to obstruct the church's original purpose. Instead of hate, which only weakens all sides, we need to espouse love by wholly accepting others.

With the church losing so many political battles, its political prominence is waning. Today, there is little political clout left to influence the government's agenda. As these political bouts continue, they draw others into protracted battles that no one wins—like the political battles being waged today on abortion and gay rights.

In the Reagan years, the Republican party adopted a big-tent philosophy that was nearly all-inclusive. They welcomed many groups, even when many of their views seemed to be discordant.

---

14   Time Magazine called Dobson "the nation's most influential evangelical leader." He is very much involved in the church's battles, lobbying Washington for ultra-conservative, backward policies.

As a result, the party's membership swelled tremendously. But as soon as Republicans began excluding certain groups, the result was a dramatic shift in support in the opposite direction and their membership declined precipitously.

What would Christianity look like today if instead the church had perpetuated a strategy of building a superior institution from the inside out and one that promoted authentic love and acceptance? I surmise that Christianity today would not have to engage a government or its people for solutions to its problems, for the church would be an overwhelming autonomous representation of the people it served.

In this country, where the Constitution explicitly seeks to keep religion out of government, why has the church found itself weighed down in so many political battles? A solution that would come much more naturally—without any fighting at all—would be to espouse tolerance of all humanity.

*If we have no peace, it is because we have forgotten
that we belong to each other.*

Mother Teresa

L et me emphatically state that when I speak of the church and
organized religion as a whole, I'm referring to the entire doctrinal
institution of religious teachings. I distinctly recount my observations
within the black church body, because that has been the more extensive
part of my experience, and I therefore reference my firsthand accounts
of events.

The black church has chosen a few ego-centered, attention-
seeking panderers to set their agenda—to lead the church. The
members revere their leaders. These leaders drive cars, wear jewelry,
and take vacations that cost more than most of those same members
earn all year.

But the advice that the church gives to its financially struggling
members is the same worn-out, dilapidated message they've always
heard: to continue praying and paying their tithes to the church
until their change come. This is of little consolation to the weary,
downtrodden members who bought into the church's message of hope

and prosperity. Preachers have not given their parishioners what they need most: love, hope, and affirmation.

Instead they distract by waddling around in issues like "the sanctity of marriage," while divorces continue to skyrocket within the church. It baffles me to see pastors and their parishioners protesting in the streets for various political issues, and then needing to have bake sales to keep the church's lights on. Personally, I've seen enough marches against gay marriage and abortion to last a lifetime, and not one march that made God or humanity better off.

I've yet to see a march or hear an outcry over the many obstacles that are *actually* plaguing the black community today, such as the lack of education and the high dropout rates. Blacks also languish in investing, saving, and other prosperity-building skills—not to mention the high number who are awash in debt. Blacks are suffering from unprecedented rates of poverty, divorce, teen pregnancy, and male incarceration.

Where are the impassioned speeches and marches about the issues that truly affect us? When will serious attention be given to the extraordinary numbers of African Americans who have no health insurance; are dying of colon, breast, and other cancers; are suffering from diabetes; are unemployed or under-employed; and are homeless? Where are all the news conferences to promote prostate screening, to promote early detection of breast cancer, to address the lack of health care in the community, and to eradicate spousal abuse and sexual molestation which usually only comes out after children are older adults? Are the primary concerns of the black church really only gay marriage and abortion?

Unfortunately, massive church gatherings and revivals do not guarantee healthcare for the underprivileged, and bake sales don't pay the members' bills at home. The church has been short-sighted, distracted by issues that do absolutely nothing to ameliorate the more pressing concerns. By ignoring these vital issues, the advancement and empowerment of African Americans has stagnated.

I'm convinced one reason that our church continues to ignore the needs of its members: it has become a haven for a lot of egotistical black men.

Black men often feel that they have to compete with their white counterparts, on the job and in social settings. But one place that a black man doesn't have to compete with whites, and can assume a role of power and prestige, is within the church. And with this role comes a newfound level of arrogance.

Today, many black churches won't allow women to lead their flocks. Many won't even let a woman walk into the pulpit area! These ridiculous, backward-facing rules of male domination only serve to keep the church, divided within itself, a male-dominated social club. It's ironic that blacks, who were the victims of discrimination not many years ago, now discriminate amongst themselves.

The implications of this discrimination are far-reaching, indeed.

Male leaders are given free rein to choose what subject matter to disseminate to the church body. Men unilaterally structure, control, and deliver the sermons they want, while they scrap sermons on subjects they find difficult or painful. Women are shut out from the discussion, relegated to menial positions in the church choir or usher board.

Can you imagine a sermon addressing the unprecedented rates of HIV infection? Would you ever hear eye-opening discussion on the down-low lifestyle? What about a talk on the molestation that happens in the church? Certainly not from the male-dominated black church. Here we have a true recipe for disaster. As long as the select few men are in charge of the church, keeping other members quiet, the issues that truly affect the church body will remain under the table. When the men in power are the molesters or victims themselves—or are living on the down-low themselves, they can choose to keep these discussions off-limits indefinitely—even until their deaths.

Not only are women kept out of power, but also, worshippers are taught not to question the male authority figures in the church, and not to question *why* women should be treated as subordinates.

This becomes a vicious cycle, stifling the intellect and paralyzing the reasoning ability of the church body. Human spirits and human lives are destroyed as a result, and it does nothing to help the church members in need. This unfruitful cycle will continue perpetually, until a genuinely enlightened leader begins to show love and appreciation for all of God's creations, elevating the church to its true calling.

Because of the lopsided state of the black church, some African Americans are finding themselves drawn to different churches: ones that were traditionally attended by whites. We find that, while not as much entertainment value is present, some white churches deliver a provocative and refreshing message, one that seems revolutionary.

Upon my first visit to a predominantly white church, the very first thing I noticed was that the offering box was placed at the entryway. Its members could leave their donation before entering into the sanctuary. That totally blew me away. How cool and unpretentious is that? This alone was a major departure from the churches I was used to attending.

Even more remarkably, the inspiring service only lasted sixty minutes—from the devotion to the benediction—and we were out the door.

—✳—

Many of my previous churches would take thirty to forty minutes of the service time just to collect the offering. Some would go as far as to call people to place their monies into the collection box based on the amount they were putting in, so that those giving several hundred dollars were called first and those giving twenty dollars or less would come forward at the end. Whether this was intended to be humiliating to those with modest donations, I don't know, but in practice, it certainly did bring a tinge of humiliation.

Other churches I attended would hand out monthly bulletins listing the monies each person tithed for the month. This would lead members to murmur during service about how much money other parishioners contributed that month. It was easy to guess what certain members earned based on their pledge to tithe ten percent. Unfortunately, this left the door open for other criticism. I remember parishioners quietly snickering that certain members must not be truthful about their tithes, that they must make lots more money than what the bulletin would seem to indicate. What's more, I remember overhearing arguments with the church secretary after she would inadvertently put the wrong dollar amount next to someone's name.

I've attended financial and deacon board meetings where more time was spent discussing the dress that sister Sarah wore to church last week than actually handling the church business. And when we would finally discuss business, tempers would often flare up because of disagreements as to how we should allot the monies given by the membership.

I have since distanced myself from the church and its confusing rhetoric and its disastrous policies. I'm more in favor of non-denominational teachings that espouse unconditional love and acceptance. I can embrace a doctrine that not only teaches we should love each other, but also teaches how to love each other. Others will continue to do the same as long as the black church continues to demonize its very members.

When I speak with my black Christian friends, I'm left with no doubt: not much has changed in the meantime: the church remains preoccupied with its gospel of greed, power, and class exclusion. The very real issues that affect its members—men on the down-low, HIV infection, and sexual molestation—continue to fester as unattended sores.

The black church is still a viable force in the community. This force could better be used to empower the underprivileged which subsequently emboldens all to seek their highest calling of authentic love. Progress is achieved through unity of spirit and diversity of talents. Collectively the entire body succeeds. We have been down this dead-end road many times throughout our history of the last two-thousand years and we should accept that exclusionary practices never get us closer to our goals—but in fact always take us further away from those goals.

In the words of Mother Teresa, "If we have no peace, it is because we have forgotten that we belong to each other."

It's difficult for some to admit that gays have always been a huge part of the church, and this remains so today. If you expand a bit to include the bisexual and transgendered, their numbers get even more significant. Now throw in those who live what's become known as on the down-low and there are not many members remaining without an identity to claim.

These parishioners worship, tithe, and lead governing committees of the church. They lead praise and worship services; they direct choirs, they play organ and piano; they lead fundraisers; they are deacons and often pastors who strive for the betterment of the church. All too often they enthusiastically embrace the very ones who are standing by to condemn them if they falter in any way.

Many will agree that some of the brightest and most gifted talents within the church are gays including married preachers. I've known those who even maintain down-low relationships on the side with unsuspecting wives not knowing or perhaps not wanting to know about their indiscretions. A reason for the secrecy is that no one wants to knowingly be hated by anyone else. The stigma associated with acknowledging a gay sexuality invite moans and murmurs of hate and contempt.

Prominent and not-so-prominent church leaders are fairly often among the gay membership. Just take a look at the number of gay preacher sex scandals throughout history and those that are still unfolding today. Even the most devout and religious among us end up in these sexual scandals. Less surprising are the number of hypocritical political leaders who advocate against gay legislation, that end up in these gay sex scandals as well. It is as though the religious and political leaders are both attempting to save themselves from themselves.

I think we should understand that we as a culture have been partly responsible for the perpetuation of the stigma attached to these social behaviors by not talking openly about our human sexuality. This silence further complicates the church's balancing act between its purported beliefs and its actual beliefs.

Our church or our religion has set our goals and expectations for us through their instructions. But many suffer in the silence of being gay and Christian, held to standards, tenets, and beliefs that are often commanding or impossible for mortal man to attain.

However, we routinely allow religious institutions to go unchecked with anti-gay hypocrisy and establish rules of morality for us to follow. It's a bit disingenuous for the church to advocate "do as I say" as opposed to leading by example. Gays cannot continue to be disenfranchised while others are made to feel superior because of their sexuality. At some point, it's more necessary to accept and embrace the ideology that *all* are worthy and tenable, that none of us are reprehensible or unworthy.

The church has become pretty accepting of its playboy celebrity status figures as spiritual and political leaders. Only the slightest attention is given to the rampant infidelity, common-law marriages, no-fault divorces, and out-of-wedlock births within the church body.

Yet parishioners eagerly rush to the pews on Sunday mornings to hear and see the pulpit used to spew hate and homophobic rhetoric— completely obliterating the Bible's frequent messages of love.

Most bothersome are parishioners who are content with sitting and listening to such vitriol in a supposedly sacred place. As a result, mothers and fathers have quit speaking or communicating with their own children indefinitely because their children have acknowledged their inherent identity as gay. They have been indoctrinated with the absurd belief that in order to love God you must hate a part of what God created. These parishioners have not only been taught to hate, but to believe that hating is in fact love.

Notably the black church has been outwardly resistant to openly accepting gays. In fact, several polls and surveys reveal that blacks, who have been rooted in the fear and non-acceptance cultivated within the church, have been the most stubborn group to accept and support any gay friendly legislation.[15] I do sense some easing in this defiant stance as many recognize it was within most of their lifetimes that African Americans as a group were considered inferior. And we are now in no position to assume a role of superiority over yet another segment of the population.

Many appeal to their higher conscience and know in their hearts that acceptance and love of oneself and others is the nature of our spirits and God, but that instinct has also been twisted by doctrines of the church and testimony of others to whom we've listened. We must love again on our own terms. I hesitate to tell someone not to listen to their teachers or preachers, but if they are not teaching authentic love and acceptance of yourself and others, then I respectfully withdraw that hesitation.

---

15   African-American men continually poll as the single group most against gay marriage. (For example, L.A. Times, June 20, 2009; Washington Post, February 28, 2011; Advocate.com, May 20, 2011.)

The illogical idea that an outside force such as the church or political laws can change human nature needs to be banished. The rhetoric of both are futile and powerless and no more capable of changing the human nature of sleeping and eating. This primitive doctrine is baseless in the consciousness of human sexuality and void of reasoning and needs to be radically challenged.

The amount of time we spend: thinking or talking about sex, planning or actually having sex confirms how much our sexuality is inherently a part of our nature. The fact that so many human sexual activities are not just for the sake of reproduction should lend credence to this belief. To suggest that one can turn off or change another's sexuality through enactment of laws or verbal condemnation with baseless rhetoric is preposterous. Once we accept that our nature is both complex and multi-dimensional, we can explore common ground to further a dialogue of individual morality.

The current state of things should lead us to question this notion that we can change or influence human nature or sexuality by spewing religious based morality rhetoric.

Gays are, and will always remain, as much a part of the church body as heterosexuals. It is ludicrous to think otherwise. It is bewildering that any religious body teaching conflicting truths would expect members to gravitate toward it. Verbally assaulting gays with hateful rhetoric and condemnation of their inherent sexuality is a colossal betrayal of the human spirit's ability to love.

Its reluctance to acknowledge our varied human sexuality is what allows the church to defend anti-gay laws of the government. This mute innocence assures that the church will eventually have to confront its own hypocrisy.

Fostering an environment of hating within the body of the church is counter-intuitive and only adds more frustrations to an already ambiguous message being purported. This issue could never be addressed with hate or intolerance, and can only be handled with love. This does not happen by condoning lifestyles of any sort, but rather a lifestyle of condoning love and acceptance.

In order for us to move beyond this ineffectual debate in the church we will need to get back to the achievable aspiration of God's authentic love. Like with other self-serving attempts to disavow others—we must embrace the highest calling of mankind to love and accept God, not the church, as the supreme governing authority of our lives.

Unfortunately, it was only after I came out of the church that I realized God's love and the church's love were two totally different types of love. Only after I accepted my own inherent nature and sexuality could I begin to comprehend the sexuality of others. The constant barrage of insults from the church encouraging me to hate myself and others like me was vastly out of alignment with God's all-encompassing love. God's love is extended unconditionally and leaves absolutely no room for doubt, questioning, or compromise!

"Life on the down-low" usually refers to males within the African-American community who have wives or girlfriends but, on the side, have clandestine sexual escapades with other men. However I find there is no racial or ethnic disparity in this group of participants based on my many conversations with those who take part in this type of sexual arrangement. Although the term down-low is usually reserved for men, it could well be applied to women as well who participate in this kind of sexual behavior.

Many living on the down-low find vindication in this title since unlike bisexual which most people consider as gay, down-low usually is taken to mean "I'm straight but I like a little same-sex action on the side." It doesn't quite carry the same tinge of contempt and deceitfulness that might otherwise apply. You most certainly won't hear preachers or politicians talking about it until they themselves are caught up in a gay sex scandal. Most of us know someone personally who participates in the down-low lifestyle.

Oftentimes the secret lovers are introduced as friends to the wife in order to make the relationship less suspect. Sitting over coffee, chit-chatting with my acquaintances, the subject has often turned to those guys who are married or sexually involved with women, but who also participate in secret rendezvous with other guys.

The majority of women should rightfully have no cause for concern, but it's surprising the number of unsuspecting wives or girlfriends who take solace in knowing that there is no other secondary woman on the side perhaps because there is no woman calling to hang up the phone when she answers. Other women who question the sexual tendencies of a partner for whatever reason are not necessarily wrong to do so: sometimes, avoiding a nagging suspicion can lead to denial or eventual heartbreak.

I've had two female friends ask me whether I thought their husband or significant other had sex with men. Conversely, guy friends have asked me if I suspected their wives were having sex with other women. In some cases they eventually discovered their suspicions were well-founded. Our suspicions alone are not reason enough to accuse another of down-low behavior. It certainly does call for us to begin an open honest discussion about our human sexuality and to stop pandering to religious rhetoric that purports to have all the answers but doesn't ask the more perplexing question: How can someone who truly loves another yet commit egregious behavior outside their moral commitment?

Now that have visited several gay-friendly cities around the world, and I live in one too, I see that such communities are frequently visited by the down-low individual seeking secret encounters. They are account executives who are away from home on business, or perhaps they are just from across town, looking for a clandestine sexual hook-up. The most unusual thing about any of this is that, back home or on the other side of town, a wife or girlfriend may be awaiting his sexual intimacy as well.

Married or committed, male friends have asked me on more than one occasion to accompany them out to a gay club or some nude male venue they had discovered. I don't go out to many clubs myself so I'm not very familiar with them, but they usually had already done the research and picked the club they wished to visit! Their usual line to lessen my suspicions was, "I'm a curious and open-minded guy." I suppose the real reason to drag me along was to act as a cover: if their wife or significant other were to catch them, they could honestly say they were just hanging out with me. Who knows how many times they had gone before they invited me; who knows how often they went afterward.

Our varying sexual behaviors across the board are nothing new. Whether asexual, bisexual, homosexual, or heterosexual, our moral compasses for acceptance are established only by the beliefs we've agreed to embrace. Our morals and beliefs are based a lot on what's taught to us (usually through religion), and they certainly don't reflect awareness of the full spectrum of human sexuality.

Still, complex questions remain unanswered: How does one demystify human sexuality? Although governmental and societal laws are broken by infidelity, are any laws of human nature broken? Our tendency to use religion as a crutch has been impotent at best. Our government's attempt to use marriage licenses and tax benefits to encourage commitment and fidelity have been trivial and ineffective. Where does our commitment to other's interpretations begin and end?

A vital step in the right direction is to acknowledge that our human sexuality is perplexing at best, and cannot be legislated by a government, regulated by rules, or explicated by religion. Superficial answers and solutions only further complicate this phenomenon with its false comprehension of mastery. Silence in the church and renunciation by our peers only heightens the false front of our stubborn ignorance to love and accept ourselves and others.

I contend that we have made the mistake of allowing government and religion to set the parameters by which we govern our human

existence. We have left the most valuable element out of the equation
—our own mind and its ability to reason. Just because government
and religion sct rules does not mean that they're in alignment with
the rules of human nature. We begin with false hopes, and we impose
these false hopes upon others if they are our sole governing authority.
The supreme Source on which you can faithfully rely is the one that
created you—and that was neither your religion nor your government.
Both those entities took a role after your arrival into the universe.
Quite simply, a government or religion cannot regulate human
sexuality—something over which it has no control.

In order to be an immaculate member of a flock of sheep one must, above all, be a sheep oneself.

Albert Einstein

I can only imagine the difficulty in reading the Bible in one hand while reading the Constitution in the other hand—let alone attempting to reconcile the two. The apparent belief some have that they are able to accomplish this task might explain why preachers are so heavily involved with politics? We even have a political entity called the "Religious Right."

I'm sure most feel they are doing a great work, however, Jesus' approach seems to have been starkly different from the approach that most take. Jesus was asked, while standing before the judgment seat of Pilate, was he the king of the Jews? In no uncertain terms, he replied that his kingdom was not of this world, and if it were, his servants would have fought to deliver him. Who knows whether or not he implied that his kingdom would ever be from here. It's more important to note that he did not choose to fight or confront as many preachers and politicians do today.

The preacher who comes across the road to play politician, especially with the intent of legislating human sexuality, should lead one to question their ability to reason or lead. No law could be created that would make a gay person straight, or vice versa.

I've known gay preachers who remained closeted within the church, while at the same time vehemently preaching in the pulpit against being gay. Some eventually left the church, while others chose to remain shrouded in secrecy. They wrestle internally with this divide while maintaining an iron-clad exterior. Some find redeeming value in publicly taking passionate political stances that condemn their own secret behavior.

For many of them, their venomous attacks on homosexuals is a therapy of the worst kind: to help suppress what they feel inside. Perhaps this cloak of secrecy may be what brings the church bowing to its knees, much like we've seen happening with the Roman Catholic church. Seemingly every week, a church leader or politician is forced to reconcile his purported beliefs with his inward beliefs, and it often concludes with his acknowledgement of being an overt homophobe who is, in fact, covertly gay.

In a 1917 paper, Sigmund Freud coined a phrase, "the narcissism of small differences," to describe our tendency to react with aggression, vitriol, and even hatred to those who resemble us the most. Freud argued that those with whom we have nothing in common cannot truly threaten us, for they are wholly "other." In contrast are those who share many but not all of our views. They threaten us because they embody the possibility that we might be wrong. Baptist Christians argue far more aggressively with other evangelicals than they do, for example, with Muslims. Wesleyans argue with Calvinists, not Buddhists.

When the scandal surrounding Bishop Eddie Long broke[16], my immediate thought was that there may at last be a prominent, charismatic religious figure in the African American community who

---

16   In case you hadn't heard, four young male members of Bishop Long's church came forward in September 2010, accusing the bishop of sexual misconduct. While a preacher being accused of sexual misconduct is nothing new, his case is particularly ironic: he has consistently spewed hateful, anti-gay rhetoric to his followers.

admits to being gay. I imagined how it would be if his massive following handled the situation with love: being accepting and non-judgmental and wholeheartedly endorsing his continued leadership. However, I was rudely dragged back down to reality when my more realistic self reminded me that there is nothing new about a gay sex scandal within the church; this too would pass, be strategically handled, and be swept under the crimson carpet of the church along with the other transgressions. It's as if the church doesn't mind its leaders engaging in this hypocritical behavior, as long as they keep it hush-hush. One merely needs to put effort into not getting caught, or perhaps into rebuking others' transgressions publicly, to keep one's own out of focus.

Bishop Long's church has enormous pull in the African-American community. It functions as much as a political institution as it does a church, having been at the forefront of nearly every recent polarizing political issue: homosexuality, abortion, marriage equality, intolerance, and fear mongering—most notably in the black community. A 2007 article in the Southern Poverty Law Center's magazine called Bishop Long "one of the most virulently homophobic black leaders in the religiously based anti-gay movement."

The moment I heard Bishop Long in his first public address since the allegations surfaced, my reality shrank. Charismatic as ever, he cunningly avoided saying he was guilty . . . but he didn't proclaim innocence, either.

He stated "I am not a perfect man." I would hope his parishioners already knew that! If they didn't, the organization is even more cultish than I would've imagined. Perhaps it is too much to ask the bishop to deny the accusations, with the same vehement conviction and self-righteousness that he usually displays when hating on others. Granted, immediately admitting guilt might not play out very well with his enormous following, so a middle ground seems most prudent for him at this time.

The reality is that the church is once again avoiding dealing with the very real issue of its secret gay society. This scandal, like countless others before it, is being yet again swept under the rug; the bishop is choosing the previously trodden path of hiding behind Biblical scriptures (and, of course, a formidable legal counsel). His scant display of wit and charm hardly insults the intelligence of committed followers, as most have become accustomed to his exhibition of power and prose.

If Bishop Long were to publicly admit to infidelity or homosexuality, would this negate all the supposed good he has done around the world? Of course not! But in the church's current state of non-acceptance, many would immediately declare him a vile, despicable man with no redeeming qualities.

What then about the church's integrity that we speak of so often in the pulpit? Is there no real reverence to be exhibited? It is my belief that whether right or wrong, guilty or innocent, it would be wise for a leader in question to step down, if only temporarily, to allow the allegations to be sorted out. Otherwise, there is a risk of further eroding the prophetic message of the church and causing irreparable damage. He adamantly chose not to stop aside. Is that not the purpose for appointing assistants and associate pastors? This would show the utmost integrity in a leader, and would be the most unselfish thing that he or she could do to allow a ministry to continue its mission without distraction.

The bishop I think would be much more respected in the end for putting the ministry before selfish desires to maintain status or egotistical motivations. A selfish decision to maintain ego comes at the expense of a faltering establishment as vibrant supporters grow weary during a distracting and public scrutiny of the ministry. Would not a parent who could not presently care for their child seek outside support to assure that the child remains nourished until they are more able to do so themselves?

I'm convinced that the flock would eventually welcome back a disgraced leader with love and open arms, no matter how these private matters play out. Besides, if the membership does not accept his return, then of course, they themselves need to recheck their own belief system and what it means to love and accept others.

Interestingly enough, Bishop Long's story was making the news cycle at the same time as a disturbing study released by the Centers for Disease Control and Prevention: black men are accounting for the majority of new HIV/AIDS infections. Men on the down-low often resort to unsafe sex with multiple partners—a losing combination. If the stigma associated with being black and gay were dissolved, how might these HIV statistics change? Those men would not resort to secret rendezvous, bathhouses, and the like. Studies have shown, over and over, that people who are open with their own sexuality are much more likely to practice safe sex.

As you can see, ostracizing gays in the church not only creates social problems, but also causes very real and very dangerous health issues. The fear of coming out in a culture built on homophobia only compounds the problem within the African-American community. Ridiculing gays will do as much to improve HIV statistics as demonizing abortions will reduce teen pregnancy, another major concern in this country and notably the black church community.

We must seek real, meaningful solutions and refrain from rhetoric that only serves to separate and cause angst and division. Sure they make for a rousing sermon on Sunday morning, but how does it help one to recognize God, strengthen Christianity, or improve mankind in any way? Those are concerns that hateful rhetoric has never and will never succeed in accomplishing.

Meanwhile a presumed innocence is granted to the revered leader, evident in how the bishop's case has already begun to play out publicly with the assumed guilt of his accusers. Most of the responses from church members have been prayers and support for the bishop. My own concern shifted to the young men who have risked being alienated by their families and others for going public with the charges. Not only will they possibly have to endure the scars of abuse for their entire lives, but they also subjected themselves to humiliation when they made their accusations public.

While the show of support for the church leadership is admirable, it makes it that much more difficult for the bishop or another leader to admit their shortcomings and begin the process of moving beyond condemnation. I'm certain that neither the bishop nor his accusers wants to disappoint their supporters or followers, but this self-entitled superiority only makes that task more difficult. The codependent relationship between the members and leader just continues to enable hypocritical behavior when forgiveness and acceptance should be eagerly waiting at the tip of each tongue and on every pursed lip.

It is not my intention to disparage Bishop Eddie Long, for he is a man of imperfection and yet perfect as we all are. In his defense, I have never attended his church, and I have never met him personally, so most references I have are from people I know who attend his church or from the accounts of his ministry purported in the media. What he seeks most right now and asked for was acceptance for who he is—not a perfect man. However, that is exactly what he has built an entire ministry on: denying this acceptance to others.

I am ecstatic about the possibility that the black church may finally be forced to confront, reconcile, and deal with tolerance of others without cowering under the crimson carpet any longer. The issue of gay acceptance is a process that the white and Catholic churches have already begun, and we must do the same. It does not matter whether or not Bishop Long accepts or admits infidelity or sexual tendencies; our highest calling should be acceptance and forgiveness and love. That said, I would certainly not wish for the gay community or any others to make a spectacle of his transgressions or shortcomings, or purport the same intolerance that he has been notorious for.

We've seen this same theater play out with several politicians and preachers who usually outwardly and staunchly oppose being gay, yet most are often masking their own same-sex desires. Over and over these self-righteous religious leaders vehemently speak against being gay and yet live hypocritical Christian lifestyles like that of Ted Haggard, Jimmy Swaggart, Mark Foley, Larry Craig, and others. This, however, has yet to play out to any significant degree in the African American community, and to date it seems to be more the white news correspondents who want to have the conversation about the denial in the black church. I was moved by the courage of a young anchorman, Don Lemon, on CNN, who openly discussed his own childhood sexual abuse on air, because the deafening drumbeat of intolerance and repudiation has dominated this conversation in the black church far too long.

The problem with mixing preachers with politics is that both sides are more often than not guilty of the very things that they accuse the other side of doing. There is no right or wrong political party or ideology that can solve mankind's real problem of creating more love for one another. We have attempted for thousands of years already using both preachers and politicians. Preachers like politicians will continue to point out the fault in others, being careful not to expose their own. If we are to transcend the religious rhetoric purported to us by both, then we must begin by seeking a spiritual solution within and not waste more time trusting a preacher or politician to lead us.

The church must be reminded that it is not the master or the servant of the state, but rather the conscience of the state. It must be the guide and the critic of the state, and never its tool. If the church does not recapture its prophetic zeal, it will become an irrelevant social club without moral or spiritual authority.

Martin Luther King, Jr.

S peaking of religion and reality, there are some things in church that I really love, that I occasionally yearn for. What I miss most is the simple enjoyment of sitting in the pews, taking in the pageantry of it all. I miss seeing all the colorful custom-made dresses and hats the ladies would wear, the tailor-made suits worn by the pastor and the men of the congregation. I looked forward to the upcoming pastors' anniversary celebrations, the big concert event of the year, and the opportunity to revel in the awe of it all, without the added cost of admission. I yearned for the sound of the angelic voices in the choir wafting through the church, and the grace of each speaker parading up to the podium to deliver their announcements—knowing that many of them had bought new wardrobes, planning weeks ahead for the opportunity to be admired.

The charismatic preaching performance would be the highlight of my morning. Afterward we'd all rush home to tell those who hadn't attended service that day about the grand performance they had missed. Church is where I felt I could have all my sins of the previous week negated once I've paraded around during the offering procession and delivered my tithes into the storehouse.

The dialogue among fellow members revolved around who could preach the most powerful message. In other words, whose charismatic and theatrical sermon would get the crowd roaring and shouting the most by displaying a superior theatrical performance.

As far as the members were concerned, many are so involved with the church and its many auxiliary clubs that their personal lives suffer from inattention. I knew members who'd attend choir rehearsal, anniversary planning, revival meetings, board meetings, and prayer meetings—in addition to teaching Sunday school.

While this constitutes a meaningful effort to serve others, they themselves are unable to keep their personal finances and relationships in working order. This misguided conditioned belief has some followers convinced that by accumulating frequent participation points, they are getting closer to, or most assuredly going to heaven— regardless of how they live their lives outside their numerous church commitments.

Although Oliver and I attend lots of local and Broadway theatre, most of them pale in comparison to the performance I'd look forward to each Sunday morning—so much so that I hardly ever attended Bible study or any of the other boring church activities that failed to deliver the jolt of exhilaration I felt when I heard the preacher whoop and holler followed by thunderous applause and standing ovations.

Outside of that, I saw little in the way of transformation or redemption in the services, and those great feelings usually lasted only as long as the service lasted, and unfortunately only ushered in the harsher reality of my everyday struggle for spirituality and a peaceful existence.

Martin Luther King, Jr. predicted, over fifty years ago, that if the church did not change, it would be relegated to a social club. Today, this prophecy is perhaps fulfilled. This leaves the church in a sad state, divided and struggling within its doors between what's righteous and what's tolerable socially. Advocating ambiguous messages of love and hate is a sure fire recipe for destroying in institution or more importantly, one's faith. This adulterated brand of religion portends its demise.

It is evident across the country that many churches are losing their sanctuaries through bankruptcy and foreclosure. There were only eight religious institutions foreclosed upon in all of 2006 and 2007. But since 2008, nearly two-hundred have been foreclosed upon, and it doesn't look like this trend is reversing anytime soon.[17] Many of these institutions were overly ambitious, aggressively seeking "megachurch" status, taking on more debt than they could repay. This was probably not the best example to set for parishioners, who watched their years of dutiful sacrifices of tithes and offering get washed away as well.

My mother has always told me that respect was not something I could demand, but instead something I had to earn. The church is no exception to that adage, and today it has a lot to earn if it endeavors to ever achieve the prestige and invincibility it one commanded.

---

17   "Churches Find End Is Nigh," Wall Street Journal, January 2011

A Wounded Caregiver: The Church in Mourning

Traditionally, the church has been a sought-after refuge in times of despair, and has for the most part done a good enough job in providing assistance to those in need. Usually, our church or our religion set the goals and expectations for us to follow. But so many of us choose to suffer, held to standards and beliefs that are impossible to wholly abide by. So what happens when the caregiver itself is wounded or afflicted and is unable to provide a loving and nurturing environment for those in need?

Any organizational body divided amongst itself, whether by class, race, or beliefs, will slowly deteriorate. This includes the church, as evidenced by the church memberships and contributors that have languished alarmingly on the sidelines of what has become more of a rebellious social club. A thriving organization will need to be supportive, welcoming, inclusive, positive, embracing, accepting, and universal if it is to continue to prosper.

This once-venerable caregiver that looked after others is now frail and wounded. Our aspiration has to be getting to know God, not recreating God to advance selfish and egotistical desires. Moreover, we must assume the ultimate responsibility for our own lives individually. We cannot hold the church responsible for deciding what is acceptable or unacceptable when the Source that created us granted each of us our own free will. If the church were to decide what is right and wrong, there would be no need for our own free will—and no need for a supreme being.

Regrettably, the church has departed from the innate belief of its leader Christ, who advocated love and acceptance on the highest level. How much time did Christ, the leader of the Christian religion, spend fighting intolerance, and how much time did Christ spend on street corners wearing a sandwich board protesting the life of lepers, robbers, thieves, murderers, and other outcasts of the day? Now contrast that with the amount of time that some Christian churches today spend protesting abortions, funerals, and marriage equality for all. This veiled attempt to recreate God in the church's image has been futile and counter-productive.

With the turmoil and mixed messages of the church, how then do we find order? Just ask the towering oak tree planted to the right of the church's front door that within lies a tiny seed. Upon landing on the ground, it only needs cultivating in order to realize its true potential. So it is with God who is within each and every one of us. Many church leaders and pastors spend years teaching about God, or teaching of God, but like the uncultivated oak seed, they remain in need of cultivation themselves. As a result, they are never actually able to teach *how* to know God.

If there's a bright side to the holier-than-thou piousness of the church, it is that members who feel accepted by God but rejected by the church will retreat in search of authentic affirmation without the preconditions required of the church. A weary soul in desperate need of affirmation cannot sit idly by, when at the very core of their being they inherently know God—and where there is God there is also unconditional love.

Not one of mankind's contributions to God, including organized religion, has been an improvement to the universe. Instead, organized religion and the church's fighting has only made more enemies and created more devout separatist classes based on ego, personal appearance and self interest. The chief message of Christ was love, a far cry from what goes on in the church today. Some religious leaders have gotten so far removed from Christ's original message that protesting the funerals of gay soldiers or the talk of abortion or gay sex is the only thing stimulating enough to engage the attention of others. This is a egregious disparity between the church leaders of today and the leadership of Christ.

Churches with so much imbalance become more obsessed with megachurch status and continuously expanding membership rolls as a benchmark of its success—rather than getting to know God. Surely there must be more meaningful ways to gather a following—ways that might actually improve the lives of mankind, or foster love and encouragement to finding the God within each of us on the basis that within our minds is the kingdom, so desperately sought.

In light of the faint vital signs of this wounded caregiver, we must seriously reconsider the lack of self-preservation that got it in this horrid condition to begin with. The question was once asked; who took Mary out of Christmas? now we should ask who took Christ out of the church?

I find it counterintuitive that any church body would advocate non-acceptance of anyone as a part of a religious belief. There are many who come into the world who are perhaps mentally unable to make what the church sees as their only rational choice. Still others out there are completely cut off because they do not fit into discriminatory rules of a religion. How do you explain that these people are going to a hell, because they can't or don't accept the church's belief? If what the church judges as acceptable or unacceptable behavior determines acceptance by a supreme being, why then the supreme being? The immediate dilemma then becomes why would a supreme being give us a unsuspecting mortal free will, and then sit in judgment, threatening punishment for exercising that very same free will?

Consider this: more than one in 2,000 children are born with a sexual anatomy that does not fit into our definitions of male and female.[18] Their ambiguous genitalia cannot be defined as male or female, while at the same time, it is both. This condition has become known as "intersex," which includes many other "differences in sex development" (DSD).

---

18   "How common is intersex?" by the Intersex Society of North America.

Just because we do not comprehend the intricacies of nature and of man is no reason to ignore or diminish the significance of their factual existence and the magnificence of God. Furthermore, knowing the complexities of gender identities, who among us is omnipotent enough to determine with which sex these individuals should identify? For the most part, this decision has been left largely up to doctors who will perform the unyielding surgery. From there, society and religion usually takes over to define and apply labels to the outcome.

To aggravate matters further, we have ignorant government policies that establish gender-biased laws that regulate marriage, partner health benefits, and tax breaks intended to assist only those who fit into its interpretation of normality. As a result some individuals are left to navigate a sea of legalities, cultural pressures and psychological reckoning to fit into an uncompromising and regressive-minded society.

How do millions of interracial persons fit into the single-identity system reflected in our laws? Birth certificates, census forms, and more require one to identify as a single race. In the higher realm of God and the universe we are, in fact, the *human* race. Where do we draw the line between the religious rhetoric that has served to keep us separated, and the vast resourcefulness of our own mind? Where does God stop and the religious rhetoric begin, and when do we shut up the nonsense and God begins?

Obviously, these are difficult questions to answer, and the purpose of this book is for us to challenge our instilled beliefs, but we should not ignore these questions or dismiss them as irrelevant because they are difficult. This is no longer about debating who we are, but accepting who we are. When human minds have been conditioned to believe that God sits in judgment of the free will they were given, it becomes a challenge to be convinced that God in fact loves and accepts them for who they are.

—✳—

I certainly do not intend to include all churches in my characterization, because many are doing a dutiful job in their community at large and around the world and have never sought to be recognized publicly for their efforts. It is wonderful to see many churches today that embrace an inclusive message of love and acceptance for all. Many of those churches go unnoticed for their many wonderful acts of kindness and selflessness and are quietly making a big difference locally and around the world.

Still, there are those whose message of love and godliness is in direct conflict with its rhetoric of exclusion and division. The dichotomies of love and hate mix together like oil and water; they cannot coexist in the higher realm of spirit. The Source, God, is love and is indivisible. Every other force in the universe can be separated into dichotomies, but to cut love in half, or take as much away from the love as you'd like, and all that will ever remain is more love. Nothing in the universe works this way except God which is love. When love is authentic, and any remnant of hate or division is added, then that source is unequivocally no longer love. There is absolutely no compromise or exceptions to this!

Whenever we and the church are connected, in right relationship with the Body of God, the Universe, we can fully embrace the unconditional love that is given each of us. Often we whittled this awesomeness down into something small, exclusive, and manageable for us and lose perspective of the magnificence of it all.

God is not cut off to us, and thus we do not need to rely on the voices of religious and political leaders to subjectively point the way toward eternity for us. The incessant desire to define ourselves by our religious affiliations is a thought we should at least reconsider. I suggest to you that the government and many religions are in fact on the wrong side of benevolence and God. To know God is to know that there is only one universal panacea in all of this, and that is the all encompassing nature and love of God.

PART V

SPIRITUAL SOLUTIONS

A man's ethical behavior should be based effectually
on sympathy, education, and social ties; no religious
basis is necessary. Man would indeed be in a poor way
if he had to be restrained by fear of punishment and
hope of reward after death.

Albert Einstein

We have been narrow-minded and irresponsible in our attempts to interpret or explain the spiritual world by using physical terms and descriptions to postulate spiritual existence. This works fairly well in the naming of physical things so that we might better communicate or relate to them, but looking to the physical world for an explanation of the spiritual doesn't make sense. Yet we resort to this line of reasoning to satisfy our need to name even that which is nameless, even though this only distorts the spiritual, in an attempt to bend it to conform to the lines of the physical.

Religion is the "belief in and worship of a faith." It usually involves a strong belief in a supreme being. It is referred to as a cultural system of powerful and long-lasting belief. "Spirituality," on the other hand, simply relates to the non-physical or immaterial. It can encompass experiences of the transcendent nature of the universe.

"Spirituality" is derived from the word "spirit," which is in turn relating to the human spirit as opposed to material or physical things. It can also refer to the ultimate reality and our connectedness with the divine realm.

Spirit and the intense affection of authentic love has to co-exist to be in-spirit. Any turning away from love, whether it manifests as anger, aggression, guilt, destruction, or fear takes us progressively away from being in spirit, or inspired. When you are "inspired", you are said to be "in spirit." This will explain the the feeling of exhilaration you get when you're simultaneously feeling total love, happiness, and blissfulness: you're at one with the universe.

Spiritual solutions are the opposite of, or perhaps the solution to, religious rhetoric. The *knowing* we inherently trusted even as we were in our mother's womb is the solution to which we must return.

First, we should understand that religion actually divides us by setting up a class of separateness that includes some but not all, it implies that all are not welcome in the group without stipulations.

Secondly, religion seeks to instruct one in a manner in which to behave or function for some intended result. Better said is that you are not encouraged to find your own inspiration of awareness, but instead you're indoctrinated and directed to follow the group.

In addition, religion seeks to control by obtaining a dominance of influential powers that mandates a codependent relationship. In other words, individual awareness and individual aspiration have to be subjected to guidelines mandated within the religious creed. The key actions here are to divide, instruct, and control, and all these actions create a resistance to being in spirit or inspired. Religion, therefore by its essence, creates a resistance to our originating all-encompassing Source.

Spirituality, on the other hand, first seeks to love unencumbered and unimpeded. That awareness alone eclipses anything most religions have ever offered, and is perhaps the most profound statement in this entire book. Secondly, spirituality seeks to encompass and include all in its path, and leaves no thing and no one out of its wake. Spirituality offers no group or class distinctions and is equally available to all without any prerequisites whatsoever. Most profoundly though, spirituality relies on enlightenment as the path to knowledge, rather than relying on instructions or lectures.

The spiritual solution for religious rhetoric quite simply is unequivocal love. There is no need for excellence in oratory skills or eloquent use of words and fancy phrases to explain love in this unrestricted context. The articulation only diminishes the encompassing nature of love, and this manipulation of the language is where the religious rhetoric begins. This love broadcasts freely, emanating like a radio station throughout the universe. Whether or not we choose to tune in, it is still present.

Religion imprisons one's mind and inherently resists love in its most uncontaminated state. Source, God, or Spirit in its most undiluted state is love. It frees one's mind. The original purpose of religion was to bring one closer to God, but has in fact done the opposite by teaching us that we are here and the Universe out there is what's happening to us. Spiritually, we are one with our Universe and what looks to be empty space between us is actually an invisible matter that connects us.

Imagine a continuum of love. On one end is the purest love; on the other end is total resistance to love. Everything in the middle represents varying degrees of resistance to love. Religion's love is not pure by its very nature of resistance to authentic love; religion's brand of love became diluted and contaminated by attaching preconditions. Sadly, this is where organized religion parts ways with the unconditional and encompassing nature of Spirit and God.

Believe that you shall receive and you shall receive.

Jesus

The powers of attraction state that, "you attract into your life that which you think about."

Several scientists, teachers, and philosophers have devoted their lives to explaining the laws of attraction, and a great many more have extensively studied and written a voluminous number of books on this subject. It is not my desire or intention to subtract or add to their dedicated endeavors. I am compelled, however, to allude to what the law of attraction represents, and how it applies to our everyday lives.

To begin, it's important to understand that thoughts are things and things are thoughts that have manifested. Even a franchise as large as McDonald's had to first begin as a thought that has now manifested. For clarification, think of your thoughts as a physical force such as wind or gravity. They are present and active although you cannot see them. Unfortunately, this law of attraction can work for both positive and negative thoughts, so it's crucial that you remain aware of your thoughts and realize that they can produce certain results. God and the universe is always and consistently emanating love and good, awaiting us to partake in much the same way through this attraction phenomena.

This power of attraction is at work in our lives, whether we acknowledge it or not, and I could write a whole book on manifesting my desires using the power of attraction alone. Whether our desire is for a spouse, a car, or a career, we can be kids in the candy store of life if we learn to apply the law of attraction. I currently have a desire for this book to be written and published, and currently I have no idea of how the universe will manifest this desire. I only know that it will. If you are reading this book in any form, then you are holding proof in your hand, of the power of attraction.

I mentioned that this law of attraction can work both ways so be specific in your thoughts. Basically you will attract what you give most attention to. If you focus on how broke you are, all you will achieve is more broke results. Let me give an example to help us better understand this law of Attraction.

A very close friend of mine called me one day in a dour mood. She was telling me about a property that she really wanted badly, but the likelihood of her getting it was pretty nil being she did not have all the financial resources to make the deal happen and several other obstacles were standing in her way that all seemed impossible to overcome. I proceded to tell her that if she really wanted this vacation property that badly, she should go about her life as though she already owned it. I asked her to bring up subjects about the property with her husband at breakfast. "Talk about the taxes on the house" "mention that you plan to plant daffodils at the front door for the spring." In other words, I wanted her to feel as though she already owned and had possession of it and was merely making plans as though she already owned it.

Several weeks passed before we talked again about the house prospects till one day she called elated to have closed on the house. Just a few weeks earlier obtaining the house seemed impossible and the reasons she gave me for her previous doubt seemed plausible to even me at the time. There is power in acknowledging things as if they were already there!

When these various laws of the universe begin working in your life, you feel how phenomenal the law of attraction is. As you continue forward on this path of allowing and accepting, you begin to expect this perpetual abundance and well-being in your life. This immense flowing of abundance is flowing at all times, and it is always our choice to allow it or resist it. Feeling good is feeling God and the presence of abundance. Our offering resistance impedes the flow of good that we are allowing to flow into our lives. This cosmic event we refer to as our life is merely our experience in the universe, and it's our freewill as to what we allow into or out of our experience.

While driving down the highway from Indianapolis to Atlanta in a brand new Ford F450 truck on my weekly visit back home for the weekend, I saw that my nephew was slumped in the passenger seat, engrossed in the fascination of the features on my new cell phone. He was thoroughly engrossed, when all of a sudden his eyes widened in amazement and he shouted, "Uncle Aaron! I see pictures of your new truck on your cell phone!"

My immediate thought was that I had just gotten this truck a couple of days before and had never taken any pictures of it. "Let me see that." I said. I motioned for the phone. Surely there must be an error, I thought as I glanced over the pictures he had discovered on my phone.

I was shocked to see the photos were of the truck that I had seen on the car lot three months ago. I remembered having been fascinated with the shiny new black truck as I marveled at it for nearly an hour at the car lot one Sunday afternoon. I enthusiastically got so caught up day-dreaming that day wanting to have that truck parked in my driveway that I ambitiously started snapping the pictures with my cell phone. I yearned for that truck, really wanting to have it in my garage, but the price was far out of my reach at the moment. Never in my adult life had I gotten so excited about a vehicle I wanted so badly. Now, along with my nephew, I was vividly remembering the child-like excitement I felt that day on the car lot. I joyfully tried to explain to my nephew the epiphany I'd had. I had attracted the very vehicle that I had dreamed into my life using the power of attraction, without even knowing those dormant powers were engaged by the universe the moment my thoughts created the knowing desire to have this truck. Just that easily, my request was granted and manifested.

That Sunday on the car lot the truck was out of my financial reach, but within the reach of the all encompassing universe. I supplied the thoughts and desires and the Source provided the rest. When the day came to buy the truck, I was able to write a check to cover the entire cost of the truck. On the day I first looked at the truck with such deep desire, I did not have the money to buy it unless I financed it which I had no desire to do. However the day I actually bought the truck I had recently gotten an unexpected influx of cash from a small company I was starting, which was starting to take off.

It has become both rewarding and exciting to utilize the power of attraction in my life by anticipating my expectations to create the manifestations I desire. As for me and the truck it was my burning desire (inspiration) to own that truck, and the child-like fascination I exhibited by taking pictures of it set the universe in motion to manifest. My excitement was similar to that of a child who desires a new bike. The child's parents, or another loved one, witnessing their euphoric desire, buys and delivers the new bike to the child. It was in the same fashion as the parents that the Universe delivered the truck to me.

We're free to use these amazing powers in the universe to manifest everything in our lives from an ideal mate, desired weight, health, friendship, vacations, and wealth, with unlimited manifestations. God's celestial store of the universe is always open and ready to deliver the desires of your heart.

Like most people, I desired a peaceful love relationship in my life. I can't say I waited, because I never anticipated when or where the universe might deliver. I did not search for, or fret over not having a romantic relationship. I only knew that in time, I'd meet the right person. It was more important for me to have a great relationship as opposed to just a relationship. I had grown to love myself so much now and no longer needed a relationship for that crutch. I hadn't given much thought to the fact that I was not romantically involved when out of nowhere romance showed up, in much the same manner my other desires and abundance showed up!

It was during a break from the Obama campaign trail when I met Oliver. I knew the instant we met that it was more than a chance encounter. It was as though time stood still for a moment, to slowly bring this awareness into focus. It was a peaceful yet euphoric moment, and I wanted it to never end. I had spent so much of my life making things go faster, even once taking Halloween hair spray to dye my hair gray in my twenties so I would look and feel as though I were older. Now I would be opting for black hairspray if I weren't bald already. However, for now, time and space paused as if to assure that I fully experienced this moment.

Little did I know that I had met someone who would inspire me to seek out the depth of my human existence here on earth. It would take a romantic interest with a hearty amount of patience and love to balance someone exhausted as I was from my previous relationships, and Oliver was the perfect person. I felt compelled to savor and appreciate the idea that all things in and out of my life had a divine purpose in play. I began feeling as if my universe had finally struck its stride like a perfectly-balanced planet rotating on it axis.

Meeting Oliver was just the beginning of a new inspiration in my life. Whatever he had that gave him such poise, I only knew that I wanted it too. The awareness that I realized within myself when around such a love-encompassing energy while euphoric was yet humbling as well. I was careful in my mind not to make too much of my feelings at the time because no matter how great it felt at the moment—I needed verifiable proof in my spirit that I was to go all in or take a more cautious approach. Granted, I had crossed paths with many wonderful spirits in the past, but none as endearing as this. I decided on seeking spiritual confirmation in my spirit which was soon after granted.

My expectation from the universe before all this was for any romantic partner to be an inspiration to me, someone for whom I might be an inspiration as well. Again that desire was granted. I truly wanted someone I could learn as much from as they might from me. Constantly praying over and over asking for something I fully believed would manifest in the first place seems quite contradictory. Therefore I never adopted the idea of mailing that letter twice. Besides, my asking and expecting so fervently that I don't ask again is a sure sign of my faith. Otherwise, repeatedly asking would convey thoughts of doubt that my desires weren't actually on their way. Just as I requested, the universe delivered precisely my desires in my meeting Oliver.

I'd never met anyone who handled himself with such poise and graciousness, without pretentiousness, as Oliver. You'd be hard-pressed to find a more thankful and inherently grateful being on the planet. The one virtue I thought I could inspire he already had, and he was there to teach me more of it.

If there was ever a spouse to inspire me to attain the life I wanted, then Oliver was just the one to assure my getting there. Fortunately for him, he did not have to do anything other than to be himself, because his poise was most natural. I was captivated observing how he handled everyday occurrences in life with ease and appreciation, and was inspired to follow his lead. I'm certain that he was not cognizant of the immeasurable impact he was having on my life and the lives of others. Before now, I had always been more confrontational and ready to offer resistance to even reason at times. My irrational logic would not play out now as it did not take many of my temper tantrums to realize that he was not buying into my nonsense. He always responded in kindness and love, and I grew quickly to appreciate his peaceful approach and confident manner of existence. I eventually learned that it's far too difficult to have an argument with an unwilling participant.

One of the most difficult things for me to grasp in my life has been patience, and I know now that Oliver was here to teach me that. Truthfully, how could such a calm spirit teach someone who could have been the poster child for a Type A personality exhibit A anything? It annoyed me at first that he had what I deemed excessive patience, which I felt conflicted with my impatience. "I know why God gave me you," I would exclaim when I felt overwhelmed . . . and he responded calmly.

He'd stare into the air as if to say, "How silly of you to be up in arms about things so unimportant." Just a few bouts with him and I soon began making a profound connection between patience and its relevance to my faith.

Being patient is a requirement of exuding faith. Things don't just happen when you have faith; patience is then required to wait for the manifestation. I subsequently became acutely aware that my exuding a vibe of patience for my desires conveyed a subtle message to the universe that I had faith, "I know you're gonna give me what I want, so I'm just waiting here until you do." The sense of expectancy was surreal but equally discerning to me. This inner expectancy was far more trustworthy than any directory or self-help handbook I had ever read.

This was a monumental shift in my awareness of the relevance of patience and faith. It took me awhile to realize that the two were interdependent. The acute awareness of this celestial interworking showed me that patience was the cue to begin the process of manifesting the expectation or knowing. The silence within the patience thereby becomes the avenue by which the Universe delivers the expectation. The process of this celestial interaction is what we routinely call faith, but this new paradigm invokes more than just a heightened belief in an expectation, but a knowing that it's no longer "if" but "when" our desires will be manifested. Consequently, we cannot have faith without having first mastered the virtue of patience.

In the course of my lifetime, I've found myself exhibiting various addictive, overindulgent behavior patterns, ranging from attending church services I didn't fully believe in, to shopping for things I didn't need and over-eating. It turns out I would overindulge because of my attitude of lack: I would drastically overcorrect in situations where I feared I might not have enough if others took too much or, heaven forbid, the universe ran out before I got mine.

When growing up, our entire family would sit around the dinner table. My siblings and I would all gobble down our food as fast as possible, often missing the pleasure of tasting it. Whoever finished first would stare down the last piece of coveted cornbread in the center of the table, hoping mom would see our plate was empty first, notice the unfulfilled expression on our face, and ration the cornbread to us. We all wanted to win that prized piece of cornbread.

It has been many years since those days at that dinner table, but the behavior and the mind-set of lack would follow me well into adulthood. After intense self-scrutiny and soul searching, I did something I call "erasing my history." I forced myself to come to terms with just how my past association of lack, even from many years ago, still had its fangs buried deep in my life today.

This was an intense process of analyzing my life today and discovering its direct connections to my past. Many will disagree with me that this is beneficial: so many are hell-bent on remembering and remaining true to their pasts at any cost. But if physically I am not the same person from long ago, why do I have to mentally and spiritually be that same person? That idea made no sense to me.

My past is just that, but my history is his-story, or more aptly put my story. Because I have control of my mind, it makes sense to me that just as I can shape my future by my thoughts, then why not reshape my past through my thoughts as well? I'm not referring to fantasy or denial, but rather to using my mind to create my own life.

If my past left me paralyzed with addictions and lack that showed up in my future and now present—and I wish to get rid of the addictions and lack—it seems like a good idea to determine where I got the assumption of lack and addiction in the past and begin there. I cannot change my parents or the country where I was born any more than I can change the color of my skin. I can, however, change the way I perceive events of the past and their subsequent role in my life.

Reversing these addictions required erasing the history that had created them in the first place, and this allowed me to create the history I'd like to have instead. I'd meditate on unlearning my conditioning, realizing that my mindset inherently evolved from my interpretation of the past. My perception could just as easily have been the complete opposite had the most minute change taken place in my interpretation. I dislike broccoli could later be interpreted as I disliked the way my mother cooked our broccoli and the list goes on.

What if I had been born in a different period, in a different country, and to different parents? How then would my life experiences have been different then they were? What if I could have written my own history? How might I have chosen for it to be played out differently?

It's easy to see how even small changes to one's history could result in a completely different worldview, and if you consider these changes and imagine their outcomes you can "erase your history"—and creatively write your own history through the power of your thoughts. "My childhood was horrible" can be later interpreted as, "my childhood was better than some".

My beliefs about myself and my surroundings were skewed greatly by my interpretation of the time and space in which I entered the universe in human form. Just like electricity, the Source is there, and we can sense the awareness of it although we cannot physically see it. The lack I once fabricated in my past does not actually exist, and in fact never existed. I interpreted a lack and that perception contributed to my relentless quest to get all I could before it would be taken by others.

This manifested a cascade effect throughout every area of my life. I'd eat more than I needed for nourishment and maintenance of a healthy body. I'd buy more car, house, or clothing than I actually needed to sustain a comfortable life. I'd futilely work more hours hoping to make more money, to spend on more things I really didn't need. This fruitless and unproductive cycle compensated for a mindset of lack that I had fabricated.

The very nature of hoarding and stockpiling can acknowledge a perceived lack in our lives. Having the awareness of abundance is precisely what keeps this abundance showing up in our lives day after day. Our abundance is manifested through excellent health, wealth, love, happiness, and a shear blissful existence in the universe. The universe, like electricity, is always delivering abundance and has no perception of lack. We don't have to see electricity to feel it—but we can see the effects of its existence by the appliances that are powered by it, the lights that switch on, and even by a bolt of lightning crossing the sky.

If we perceive lack, then the universe cannot respond to those thoughts. It does not know what lack is, because lack is not a part of abundance. Our Source only deals in abundance, and nothing else. As we begin to understand that, we quickly realize that there is absolutely no need to overeat, over shop, over work, or worry at all about being provided for.

Birds do not worry where their next meal is coming from, yet God makes sure that every one is fed. Animals do not fret, shopping for a new winter coat, yet this abundance of the universe provides them one at precisely the right time when winter shows up. It is futile for us to worry about the beating of our hearts or kick-starting our organs each morning upon awaking, because God's abundance nourishes them day and night with no effort or acknowledgement on our part.

Given that we take most of these things for granted, it stands to reason that we over-consume and worry about such minuscule things. It's up to us to make a hell of this heaven we live in or in fact a heaven of our hell while here. We would be best served by building a rapport with our universe which equates to our favor with Source and God.

We have to banish the belief in lack that has been pounded into our minds in the past. Abundance means abundance. It does not run out for one person simply because another has received it. We are an extension of this vast universe, and there is no threat of there not being enough for me regardless of how much you and others take, and vice versa.

The prevailing belief that people like myself who come from poor backgrounds never get to enjoy profound pleasures in life, because they were not born into them, is false and deceiving. Anyone can harvest this Source of abundance in the universe through intentionally allowing, expecting, accepting, and receiving what is inherently ours. We have to acknowledge that we are already in possession of the abundance we desire because we are. It is not necessary to understand how this celestial orchestration works, just know that it is working without ceasing, whether or not we believe it—and whether or not we understand or partake of it.

t was a Christmas morning when I was about twelve years old that my
mom had taken us all to my grandmother's house to celebrate the holiday
with our extended family. My siblings and I played in the yard all day on
Christmas Eve with my cousin Stanley, an only child of my aunt and uncle.
I was glad to be away from Cocoa, the small town we lived in. Family
vacations of any sort were rare—we never had much extra money, and mom
getting eleven kids into our station wagon was a feat in and of itself.

My siblings and I eagerly anticipated Christmas morning, sensing
that this Christmas would be different from all the others where we
only got perhaps one toy, or more likely, a toy to share. My father had
died a couple years earlier at age forty-one from the stroke related to
his high blood pressure. It had been particularly hard on just my mom
raising eleven kids alone, and it should have been considered a present
enough just to get us all one hundred and fifty miles away from home
to Jacksonville, Fl. for the holiday.

After the darkness of Christmas Eve started to fall, we were
summoned inside the house to have our baths and get tucked into
bed by grandmother. I was so full of glee and anticipation that I found
it unbearable to try and sleep. I eagerly awaited for what I envisioned
would be a wonderful Christmas morning with toys and gifts strewn
all over the living room floor.

We got up early Christmas morning along with our cousin Stanley and ventured into the living room to find Mom, Grandmother, my aunt, and my uncle sitting and conversing around the tree. My wildest dream seemed realized when I found what I had anticipated—what seemed like hundreds of toys and gifts under the Christmas tree.

The gleeful feeling and ecstasy vanished as quickly as it had arrived when we immediately found out that of the countless wrapped gifts, nearly all were for my cousin Stanley, and only four or five out of the pile belonged to the eleven of us.

We opened our shared gifts rather quickly, and spent what seemed like an eternity watching Stanley open present after present and relish his new bike, games, and toy trucks. I soon began sobbing uncontrollably because my cousin Stanley had everything, and I had nothing I thought. I rarely cried as a child, but the grief was too much for me to bear!

Mom tried to question me as to what was wrong, but I could not talk and cry at the same time to answer her. It was quite a few moments before I could bring myself to answer her question, "What's wrong with you, boy?" she asked. I choked back the tears and muffled my cry just enough to angrily exclaim, "I want to be like Stanley!" After all her attempts to verbally console me, it took my noticing what looked like shame, but probably more embarrassment and hurt in her facial expressions—to quiet me long enough to hear her crackled voice apologize for my sudden anxiety.

Now, having raised a couple of kids myself, I can only imagine how hurtful this must have been to my mother, who was doing the best that she could, given the gravity of her situation in those lean years. She was single-handedly rearing eleven kids—and we were all born within a seven-year span, since she had three sets of twins within a three year period.

Of all of the hurtful things my kids have managed to act out, none has compared to the selfishness and ungratefulness I displayed with my mother that Christmas morning. It was a few short years later that my selfish and ungrateful actions would come full circle to my own awareness.

We got word that Stanley had been jailed on murder charges while yet a teenager. He was charged and eventually convicted of killing someone during an attempted robbery. He would serve the first several years of his adult life in prison. He was released after completing a ten-year sentence, only to attempt another robbery—but this time it was he himself who would be killed during the burglary.

That was a long time ago it seems, but there are very few days that I don't reflect on those words I angrily hurled at my mother. "I want to be like Stanley." There are profound lessons in this message that still stick with me this very day. Gratitude for even what seem to be unanswered requests is a virtue we should all espouse. We have to be grateful for all things in and out of our lives no matter our perception.

Do I still want to be like Stanley? Absolutely not. I only want to be the Aaron that God made and created me to be.

W e've not owned a television for several years, and by this point in my story this probably isn't a huge surprise.

In the house we lived in before now, there were thirteen televisions throughout the house, even in the bathrooms. At the time I felt drawn, compelled, and even obligated to watch all the depressing news and headlines from around the world. With a television in every room, I was assured I'd never miss any unsettling events that happened around the world. I especially delighted in breaking news because I might be first to spread the miserable news to those the correspondents may have missed: like my family and friends.

Like many Americans in 2001, I too was fixated on the news coverage of the September 11 World Trade Center attacks. I was drawn to the horrors that the media portrayed. I was obsessed with their reports of what was happening a thousand miles away from me. I'd flip through channels searching for pundits and correspondents, eagerly giving their accounts and assessment of the ongoing catastrophe. My brain eagerly awaited my news fix each day, which would make me feel bad or good, depending on the turn of events.

Several months later, during a routine check-up, I described to my doctor my inability to sleep, and explained my not being tired enough to sleep for more than two hours each night. After stating my case, he cross-examined me, and I found myself defending my addiction to the news like an addict might, after running out of drugs. The final diagnosis was that my media-induced addiction to horrible news was the reason I was staying awake instead of sleeping.

I took the advice to silence the news without hesitation, for I was fatigued and delirious from months of limited sleep. This immediate relief of being able to sleep again served as a catalyst for purging my addiction to negative news energy, and thoughts perpetuated by the media. Little did I know the profound awareness this experience would eventually bring me—and that I'd have the relief of being able to sleep without recurring nightmares of planes flying into buildings or towers collapsing, and people jumping to their death out of 52nd story windows. More importantly, I was forced to examine the effects of the materials I was filling my mind with. That act alone allowed for more positive thoughts to flow into my mind and subsequently my life.

Although I did not swear off television immediately, it was apparent that my media addiction would be short-lived, as the positive thoughts and energy were becoming my new drug of choice. I began to view my mind in the exact way I viewed my body, and I started feeding it nourishing and life-sustaining nutrients. Just as I could not expect anything wonderful out of a body that I continued to pollute with poison and filth, so it is with my mind. Likewise, how could I have expected to view life in a positive manner, or experience a blissful life, if I gorged on trashy and depressing, condescending news perpetuated by biased news commentators and correspondents relying on spin to increase their advertising revenue from their affiliates? The media rewards those who produce the most effective spin and therefore generate the most viewers and revenue, and this trend has become increasingly disturbing in light of all the political propaganda we're forced to decipher.

—✳—

At age thirty-two, my weight mushroomed from 172 to 215 pounds within one year before I even took notice that it had changed. I had so embraced the life of reluctance to do anything more than enough to get by. My food addiction had become my drug of choice for numbing my feelings of under achievement. Being able to buy food and eat out often made me feel adequate and accomplished.

Within three months I had lost the weight and was again at my normal weight, and never suffered that kind of weight gain again. My response has always been the same, and I won't vary now. I created this mantra for myself years ago and apply it still today in different areas of my life. I hope it brings you the same results that it has yielded me without the use of pills or temporary fixes.

Here it goes. The best way to lose weight is to not gain any weight. That is it—plain and simple. This simple way of thinking can apply to all areas of your life. If you don't want to smoke, then I suggest you not start smoking in the first place. This proactive approach can apply to drinking, gambling, or anything we choose to not do. Most definitely, this will circumvent any new or additional habits that you might pick up. If you can create this thought process as your mindset, you will find that you will first subconsciously and then consciously quit habits you've already started. If you're already overweight, than the mindset of not gaining anymore weight will effortlessly cause you to lose weight as you focus on not gaining weight. This will break habits your mind thought you had.

As you embrace this mindset of being a healthy weight, totally in tune with your universe, you will find yourself exercising naturally, perhaps by taking the stairs when you would have usually taken the elevator. You will notice that, without much thought, you start to put less food on your plate. You might even find yourself enrolling in a yoga or tennis class. I started with small, incremental changes like these, and today by choice I don't eat beef, pork, or poultry. At least for now, I do maintain seafood in my diet. In addition, I eat plenty of salads and vegetables, which make the majority of my meals. I hike, bike, and practice yoga regularly. I also gave up my car since I live in a walkable city with a subway system. Most of all, I've trained my mind to only eat if I am hungry, independent of the times others are eating or when society dictates I should eat.

Keep in mind that your mind is a powerful resource and you should take advantage of its capabilities. As you begin looking at your mind and body in the context of not putting anything into it that will pollute it, that will enhance your efforts tremendously. Successful weight loss and maintenance have more to do with mindset and desire than any of the countless diet plans available on the market.

Lastly, remember that to conquer habits and addictions, we not only need to quit them, but also replace them with the habits we wish to form.

There seems to be a lot of talk about change in our world today. We're told that if things aren't as we like, we should change them. For the most part I agree. However, a line gets drawn in the sand when the mantra of change crosses over into attempts to change the human awareness and spirit. I'd much prefer the more natural-feeling state of Source awareness that embraces living the *here* and *now* as opposed to the culmination of suffering, redeemable for some future event. In my case change was a good thing.

Oliver and I anxiously awaited our move out of our five-bedroom home and eagerly anticipated the move into a one-room basement apartment. We wanted desperately to be rid of the accumulated "stuff" that no longer enhanced our lives in search of a more meaningful existence of less is more. We loathed the shackles of homeownership and unneeded possessions, and yearned to get rid of the nonessentials in our lives. Besides we both loved to travel and that seemed to be a much better use of our resources than dumping them in a big house.

It's difficult to imagine the amount of change that took place in a matter of a few months with our focused commitment and concentration on simplifying our life. In the midst of all the wrangling I found myself enthralled in a spiritual journey that I had neither prepared for nor would have known how to prepare for had I anticipated it. All the dormant forces in my world seemed to come together all at once to allow our desire for simplicity to fall in place.

In just the previous year we had traveled to more places than most people in their entire lives. We, like many others, had been caught up in the fascination of the election of Barak Obama—a major milestone in that he was the first African American president—but for me the journey had begun a long time ago. Truthfully, I was not aware it had begun until I suddenly realized that a sense of contentment had come over me—something I had never experienced before.

As I was letting go of things I had strived to attain for most of my life, I was replacing them with things I really did want in my life—namely the loving companionship I now had with Oliver, along with a simplified and low-stress lifestyle. We had a nice car but wanted a simpler car, or better yet, no car. Now we could manage not having a car even by living in the city. The yearning desire for simplicity had taken over the dreaded distresses of anxiety, fear, and constant mayhem.

I briefly imagined family and friends thinking that we had gone nuts, but those concerns stopped as I felt this of purpose and reconnection with the universe. By this point, I strongly felt that less was in fact more.

If we didn't have possessions like cars or houses, there would be no need to provide maintenance or upkeep for them. Most importantly, we would have no need to worry about the safety or insurance of things we didn't have. My heightened sense of awareness was a humble catalyst for coming to terms with my newfound reality. It allowed the serenity I needed to write this book.

After living in a one-room basement apartment on the outskirts of D.C., we started to yearn for roots and stability within the city we were quite fond of. Our dilemma was that we had no interest in buying another house that would bog us down in captivity, and we were reluctant to rent with no control over rising rental costs. It'd be a difficult compromise, but we didn't yield on either point.

A short time later, after having dinner with friends, we decided to prolong the evening by all joining up at a late-night crêperie for dessert. While waiting for our order to be prepared, my friend girl got a call on her cell phone, and through the course of her conversation I overheard her discussion about the sale of a co-op that was coming available in the city.

After she'd hung up the phone, I enquired enthusiastically about the co-op, and where it was. She suggested that if we were interested, we should apply immediately for a membership and she gave me contact information as well.

Neither Oliver nor I really knew what a co-op was at the time, and had only heard the term used, but had no clear understanding of the concept. We all parted for the evening, but first thing the next morning we began investigating the opportunity to buy in the city to which we had grown so attached. After a few phone calls it was apparent that if we could pull it off, then this would be the opportunity of a lifetime— and the answer from the universe to our housing dilemma.

The co-op would offer us what had seemed like a ridiculous request before now. It would allow us a place in the city we loved and wanted so much to be a part of, and the freedom from skyrocketing rents. Most of all we would own, without the stresses of ownership and maintenance. The thought of such an option had never entered our minds, yet the universe had seen to it that our far-fetched request was dropped in our laps, in the form of a friend's overheard conversation.

Three months later we received word that we were unanimously approved by the board. An amazing synchronization of events by the universe had taken place before our eyes while we were merely observers of this celestial orchestration of events being manifested on request. An opportunity neither of us had known existed a few months before was now completely within our reach, and our minuscule role was simply to observe and not to impede the flow.

Comfortably settled in, we're elated that our home feels very much like checking into a well-kept hotel most any time. We're able to travel to faraway places or visit family and friends without the frustrations of continual house maintenance. We have housekeeping and laundry service provided and are just a few steps away from most any dining option we choose. I mention these things in the hope of inspiring others to nurture their minds to expect the rich rewards and abundance available to all in the universe.

Possessions are wonderful things when we can actually enjoy having them or they enhance our lives in certain ways. Stockpiling or hoarding for the sake of pleasing or competing with others is an egregious waste of energy that keeps us from the higher realm of living in Spirit where we have a treasure trove of resources consistently available to us so there is no need to squander.

Like many others, I faulted stress for my weight gain, and have shared the frustrations of those struggling with the issue of their weight before realizing that stress was not something you could quantify. I regularly referred to the term in describing the state of being I was feeling at any given time. I know now that stress is not something you can get a measurement of to determine how much of it you have or had, as you can with a blood sample to see how much sugar is in your blood. Stress therefore, is nothing physical although it can produce physical symptoms. Stress is merely symptoms of our reaction to or interpretation of a particular event. We manufacture our own symptoms when we process certain thoughts as stressful through our thinking.

Stress is perceived only in our minds as something we have possession of, and yet it cannot be bottled up, measured, or contained as we are taught to believe. You can go to the doctor to check your cortisol level, which tends to go up when you perceive an event as a threat or stressful, but that is not stress itself. You will not be able to get a quantified test of how much stress you have in your body and blood at any time, so let's put this myth to bed and realize that it is our interpretation of events in our life that we perceive as stress or not stress. That is why two people can experience the same event and have completely different reactions—they merely react to it differently.

Even having gained more than forty pounds and three pants sizes, I was oblivious to the fact that I had gained even one pound. I went about each day of my life working and doing what I thought was getting me ahead, even if that meant inadvertently crushing others to get there. To reward myself and feel deserving for completing the struggle of working all week, I would cook, eat, and drink all weekend to bury the agony of commencing the cycle again on Monday.

On a more adventuresome Saturday morning I drove down to meet up with my brother for a weekend in Fort Lauderdale, three hours away. It had become habit to meet up at a restaurant as if to celebrate the drive down. As usual, he navigated me by cell phone to a restaurant he had chosen for our meeting. When I pulled up across the street to park my truck, he eagerly awaited me and waved to acknowledge my arrival. He watched with anticipation as I exited my truck and crossed the street to greet him. We said our hellos and entered the restaurant to get seated and order our food. Midway through our conversation, my brother in his usual candid and comedic manner exclaimed, "My God, you looked like a Butterball turkey crossing that street to meet me. What in the world happened to you? I almost didn't recognize you!" The verbal assault continued, "Wow! I've never seen you fat before, and it just looks funny!"

That was the very first time in my entire life I'd ever been called "fat" by anyone. Up until then, and particularly during the previous year, I had not given a second thought—or cared enough—to take notice of my weight. I was struggling with an anemic business venture, having to deal with a rebellious teenager at home, and trying to maintain an unfulfilling marriage as well.

It was not until I got back home that evening that I weighed myself and found out that I had eclipsed 215 pounds. I felt so ashamed that I immediately started a diet and exercise program that same night as I drove back home by not stopping for my usual late night snacks.

The next morning at home, I spent thirty minutes getting ready for my first run through my neighborhood. Unfortunately that run would only last about six minutes before my heart would start racing and pounding so hard that I felt it would jump out of my chest any moment. I had never really run nor exercised in my entire adult life, because I never realized the need to. My ambitious plans were foiled as I was forced to retreat back into the house and catch my breath. I quickly regrouped mentally and opted for a less aggressive approach to my mission. Within three months I had lost fifty-five pounds and gotten down to 160 pounds. With dire dedication I had lost the weight so fast that I looked skeletal to even me, and eventually I achieved a healthier weight of 175 pounds, and never again had a significant weight problem. If I could now do without so much overeating, what made me think I needed to overeat to begin with. The subtle change and acceptance started to take place in my mind.

Weight loss and maintenance has more to do with our mindset than a diet based on what we should or shouldn't eat. A positive mindset supersedes even a rigid exercise routine one might undertake. I'm convinced my own weight loss, 100 percent, was due to my mindset—not to the controlled eating and exercise I was doing. I've discovered that by using the same mind-based principles I've used in other areas of my life applies here as well.

So why not start in the mind to eliminate any stressful or harmful behavior? We would certainly be resolving the issue at the root cause where it started and be assured of eradicating its beginnings. Although I've done some extensive research in that area, I am not interested in advising on how to lose weight, because that is not my area of expertise, and there are others more qualified to do so. I will, however, reference a few comparative observations I used to guide my own thoughts.

First of all the earth is 70 percent water, our body is 70 to 80 percent water, so might this suggest that our diets should consist of 70 percent water through water-laden fruits and vegetables?

Secondly, our stomach is about the size of our fist, indicating that our body would be able to get sufficient nutrition in that amount of space to sustain life, so how much does our belief in lack contribute to the acceptance of the belief that we should consume more than the body intended naturally? I would consider whether this behavior is learned or conditioned, and then govern oneself accordingly.

Thirdly, consider having more awareness about eating by making a mind-body connection while eating and listening to the body while consuming foods. Use this consumption time to enjoy the sensations of the many taste capabilities of the tongue after all they're there for that reason.

Notice that all three of the things I've mentioned have to do with your mind awareness, and none are suggestions to count calories or monitor food intake. What I found is that as I internally began the awakening and awareness process in my mind, healthier habits started to take form, almost miraculously. I found myself without effort avoiding sodas, exercising regularly, participating in yoga classes, and making other confirming lifestyle changes—as long as I listened to my body.

Lastly, recognize what you perceive as stress and what you're reacting to in a stressful manner. I repeat also that if you don't want to deal with having to lose weight again, then be proactive by not gaining any weight. These principles will guide you to an awesome appreciation of your body, the temple provided to house your spirit here on earth.

Hanging onto resentment is letting someone you despise live rent-free in your head

Ann Landers

had a big disagreement with my daughter one day. She ended up getting pretty offensive in the language she was using to try and persuade me to sense whatever she was feeling. It started when I had tried to initiate a conversation about her recent series of emotional rants that seemed to come out of nowhere. Regrettably, I ended up having her escorted away—but I am thankful that it ended the tirade.

One thing stuck with me most that day: I saw in her the same nasty temper and demeanor that I once harbored myself. It made me question why anyone had associated with me at all during those years so much anger and resentment boiled beneath my skin. And it made me finally understand what my mother may have felt when, nearly thirty years ago, I treated her similarly. But as angry and hateful as I felt my daughter was acting that day, I'm sorry that she could show only a combative attitude in the face of the peace I was offering. I know that the intense energy she was using to "hate" me was actually proof that she loved me very much.

—✳—

I'm proud of my reaction to her furious ranting and lashing out about what a horrible person and father I was. Responding to anger with kindness was definitely vital in the situation. It was now my time to perform against this hostile backdrop. The entire episode of fury was about me learning as much as it was for her. I was just weeks away from the start of a major book tour and at a relatively high point in my life and career. Her repeated attempts to drag me into her hostile behavior took me right to the abyss of counter-confrontation, but only that I may remember the view, and remember my own past behaviors I talked about in the *Out of Control* chapter. I would not join in her hate parade no matter what buttons she attempted to push.

Nearly thirty years earlier, I was the one standing across town yelling and pleading to be shot, having forgotten completely about my two young children back home. The striking parallel was that it was she, now, who was hell-bent on making a scene that she completely forgot about the wellbeing of her own two children, knowing that if she was asked to leave, they would have to go with her. But just as my ignorance taught me, it was now time for her out-of-control temper to enlighten her as to the thoughtless results of being vengeful and ungrateful.

When she would leave me hateful voice or emails I'd immediately delete them without reading or listening past the first couple of negative words. It was in her heated moment of despair that reality got muddled in the smoke of her hatred and anger toward me. I was intent, however, on sending only love and peace into her life—things she needed more than anything material I could have given her.

I've learned to accept and appreciate all the lessons in my life, and this was no exception. The night before the altercation, as I lay awake in bed unable to sleep, anticipating the next morning when I would have a serious conversation with her about her recent behavior, I was unaware that I was also creating a low-energy vibration that would conflict with hers, ultimately causing us to clash.

I was being booked for radio talks, book signings, and readings around the country. These talks would be about espousing love, peace, and acceptance. I was amazed by my own poise in handling her anger at me. My life had been quite drama-free for several years, and now just before my first book launch I was forced to meet an ultimate test to validate the words I'd written in the book. Given that the underlying message of the book was love and acceptance, it was paradoxical to ask her to leave. However, it is in total love that I would not own her hate, but instead allow her to grow and flourish without me as a crutch, to learn her own lessons as I had done. The only thing that matters now is how she and I both can grow and learn from this experience.

Thinking back to the series of events that led up to the fight, I realize that we all have to find our own way back to love. This comes by constantly seeking a higher awareness as the observers of our lives—rather than being trapped in the physical, material compositions that we've come to think of as ourselves. Life is happening everyday around each of us and we observe it in other things and oftentimes in each other. But until we can become the observers of our own lives, we exist in a state of despondency—with an attitude that we are helpless in our world, with little influence over the things that happen to us.

Portland, Oregon. August 2007.

was taking my regularly scheduled cross-country drive. I was also using this vacation as a time to scope Portland out, given that I had heard and read so many wonderful things about it. I was seriously considering moving there, after determining that it was time to leave Atlanta. Sure enough, the city has most of what I'd dream of having for a backdrop—the combination of mountains near Mt. Hood, and lots of water ways near the city center.

As I anticipated, the city did not disappoint. After enjoying a delectable dinner and an evening of drinks and conversation with other visitors I had met while at Jake's Famous Crawfish a block from the Mark Spencer, where I was staying for the week, I meandered back to the hotel.

As I walked into the lobby, I was flagged by the clerk at the front reception desk, whom I now knew on a first name basis, to retrieve a message left for me. "Thanks," I said as I took the message and turned to walk the three floors up to my room. Looking at the note, the name and number on the message were not recognizable to me. I pondered for a few moments before calling the number from my cell.

The male voice that picked up on the other end had a slight accent, and he proceeded to tell me after minimal questions that he was my sister Eartha's doctor, and that her organs were shutting down, the result of colon cancer she'd been fighting for years. He needed me or someone to sign for her to be admitted to hospice so she would get the best care just before her death.

I made no follow up calls to anyone, and to this very date I have not met that doctor, nor do I know who he was or how he ever got my phone number or located me all the way in Portland, while she was thousands of miles away in a Florida hospital.

Granted, we all knew my sister had been dealing with cancer and other complications for the last several years, but somehow she had managed to keep her spirits and all those around her high while confidently speaking matter-of-factly about her terminal illness. The family had grown accustomed to her going in and out of the hospitals frequently over the last several years, so it was not unusual for her to be there, but this time was different. I don't think any of us had the doctor call us with such dreadful news or ever truly anticipated it, given that she was always so assuredly in control through all the pain and suffering she endured the last several years of her life. In any regard, I would be cutting my vacation short and heading to Florida to be near her during this time. I could not be any further from Florida if I were anywhere else in the country at that moment.

After I debated flying and leaving my car in Portland, or making the 3200-mile drive to Florida, I had decided on the latter, given the time involved with layovers and waiting in airport terminals as opposed to just driving straight through. Besides, I could use the alone time to reflect on my impending reality. Long before dawn the next morning, I loaded the car and set out without hesitation for a long journey south. In light of what was going on in my head, the drive and everything else seemed trivial. Once I cranked the car up that morning, I would stop only for gas over the next 3200 miles.

—✳—

After nearly 48 hours of only stopping for gas and snacks, my first stop for rest was around 5:00 AM at a rest area between Daytona Beach and Cocoa Beach, Florida. It was the first time I remember exhaling, knowing I was less than an hour from my eldest sister. I pulled in to shut my eyes and give the hospital patients time to wake for breakfast.

Two hours later the sun began creeping through the car windows and awakened me. I drove in a beeline to Wuesthoff Memorial Hospital to see and hopefully talk with my sister in what must be a surreal experience for us both. It was difficult knowing the doctor had already spoken with her about her impending death. I knew I would have to be a trooper in all of this for her sake and not mine, not to mention that I was completely oblivious to my own existence at this point.

—✳—

After getting a visitor's badge and being directed upstairs, I walked in not knowing what to expect. My mind bounced between expecting a miraculous recovery, while also preparing to accept the worst. When I walked in at about 6:30 am, I found her room to be very peaceful and quiet. There were no other guests in the room. A breakfast tray had already been delivered to her bedside and was starting to get cold. She appeared way too weak and frail to feed herself, though perhaps she wanted to eat.

It was when I walked to her bedside that her eyes immediately welled with tears and she began to cry. I asked her about her hunger and pain levels, and she mumbled in a low voice that she wanted to eat the oatmeal and that she wanted the cranberry juice. She gently instructed me on how to fix her oatmeal the way she liked it, and I followed her requests to the letter. At first I tried handing her the properly prepared oatmeal, and she politely told me that I would have to feed it to her, and gratefully I did just that. She than directed me to the straw to put in the cranberry juice so that she could sip when I put the straw to her lip, and again I felt grateful to assist.

It was somewhere between the spoonfuls of oatmeal that I was feeding to her that I felt compelled to politely bring up the phone call I had received back in Portland from her doctor, only because the doctor had urgently warned me that delaying a decision would make end of life more difficult for her and the family if those papers did not get signed ASAP.

I would have opted not to bring it up at all. His admonishments to me were her major organs that had not yet shut down were just about to, and that if she expired without the agreement then hospital policy would be to attempt resuscitation, which could leave her with broken ribs or in a vegetative state. His suggestion was to admit her to hospice for a dignified death with our family members close by to say our goodbyes. Either scenario seemed too difficult to handle.

"You know your doctor called me, don't you?" I asked her.

"Yes," she said while nodding her head in the affirmative. "He wants you to sign those papers," she went on to say.

Through the agony of all this, I felt slightly relieved to bring this conversation past our lips, and I truly believed she felt that way as well. I went on to voice my concern that I only wanted to sign those papers if she agreed with doing so. Again she said "yes," while nodding in the affirmative, but seeming more reluctant than before, or at least not interested in discussing it further. I can only imagine what thoughts were on her mind that very moment.

By this time I could not continue a line of questioning that seemed like torture to us both, and abruptly I changed the conversation back to her pain and hunger levels, and finished feeding her breakfast. She went on to ask me about both her children and other family members. I told her that I had heard that her daughter was on the way and I had not seen her son since arriving in town.

Moments later, her nurse walked in and asked if I was her brother Aaron and whether I would join her in the hallway when I got the chance so she could give me the "Do Not Resuscitate" paperwork to look over before signing. I obliged. When I stepped outside the door, she explained the paperwork in a scripted, matter-of-fact manner as though she had been through the routine many times before, but as if there was some urgency in doing so. I'm not sure whether her anxiety for a signature was because she finally had a family member to sign the paperwork, or that my sister's impending death was moments away.

Suddenly, I looked up, and asked for more time to discuss this with her children and other family members. With frankness, she looked me directly in the eye and said, "There is not much time to decide, so you must make it quick." I went outside into an empty space I found in the hallway and immediately began trying to contact family members to make them aware of what we were up against. Understandably, this type of news could never be easy for anyone to take, and making a quick and multilateral decision with such a large family would be difficult—even with plenty of time to discuss.

I called several family members and got responses like "I will have to call you back to let you know what I think," or "You should call so-and-so to see what she thinks." It was then I knew the frustration the doctor had expressed on the phone was because no one wanted to make a decision, and a decision needed to be made soon. I inherently knew my reason for being there at that very moment was to watch all this unfold, by myself.

I had visited Eartha a month earlier at home, at a time when her hospice nurse came by for a routine visit to distribute her meds and discuss her prognosis. I tried to leave the room to give her and the nurse their privacy, and Eartha had waved for me to not leave the room, and then made eye contact with the nurse and told her that everything they discuss, I should hear. She wanted me to hear and know everything.

I know now that she was preparing me in case I had to assume the role of guardian, in her unique and lovable way of accomplishing major things with subtlety.

A couple of days after she went to the hospice wing of the hospital, I climbed in the bed beside her and caressed her face. I told her how I loved and appreciated her for her commitment to our family. I went on to tell her it was okay for her to get some rest and not worry about leaving us anymore, I knew she was concerned about leaving us, because she was so dedicated to the whole family.. I said my goodbyes, left the car at my mother's house, and headed to the airport for a flight back to Atlanta.

The moment the plane landed at the Atlanta airport, and was taxing toward the gate—I turned on the cell phone and realized I had several voicemails alerting me of my sister's passing. I remembered reading somewhere that love is not as complicated as we think; it is only difficult when we don't love.

Eartha had visited me in Atlanta on several occasions, and she had even managed to make it to my last birthday party before she died.

She did most all of the preparation, as I was busy entertaining Franz, a friend who had flown in earlier from Italy to join in my celebration. All her adult life, we all heard her speak repeatedly of her love for Italy, for the Italians, and for their cuisine. She applauded their style in clothing and design. Although she had never gone to Italy, she had an instinctive attraction to exceptional and fine things.

I take solace now in several things that went on during that last visit—things that I paid little attention to at the time. I'm grateful for

Franz, because she immediately connected with him and before the night was over they were calling each other brother and sister. She must have prodded him for every detail of life in Italy.

As sick as she was, the excitement of chatting with Franz, who spoke fluent English, allowed her to never let up with the food preparations and organization of the party events. Secondly, I know how much she labored to make my birthday the huge success it turned out to be, even though she was in pain. I only knew of her pain later that evening when the guests had started to arrive and the party was getting started. I peeked into her room to ask if she was ready for the party, and she bravely smiled and said "not tonight, but I want you to have a happy birthday."

Meanwhile, she was holding on to her side, obviously in excruciating pain. It affected me greatly that she sat out the party in so much pain, but I know in her heart because it was a pleasure for me, it was a price she gladly paid. She braved so much just to spend more precious time with us. She dedicated her life to making others happy that day and especially me. I'm ever so grateful to be still receiving her happiness and love even today.

I asked the question in the first chapter of this book: Where were you or I then? Where are you now? Often I ask that very question of Eartha . . .

I know that your body you wore on earth weighs exactly the same as before you left, I know also that you are no longer there . . . Are you those stars that twinkle at night? Are you the sunshine that brings earth its light . . . or rather the moonlight that watches over the night? I know for sure that you are still here, for I behold your presence forever so near.

If you have a particular faith or religion, that is good.
But you can survive without it.

Dalai Lama

Writing this book—about reuniting mankind with its intrinsic Source of love—has been a fun, exciting, but formidable undertaking for me. At many times in the text, the altruistic attitude and way forward I espouse seemingly conflict with my own beliefs and interpretations. The subject matter may appear judgmental . . . at least on the surface.

Some may find parts of this book hard-hitting and direct. Admittedly it has not been an easy task to talk on what is sensitive and very personal subjects for many, but a bad tooth hurts until it is pulled. Once cooler heads prevail, let's remember that the ultimate objective of this book is to promote love and acceptance within our society at large. In fact, it is my earnest intention to initiate an awakening and reckoning in each of our minds, to invoke the courage to control our own lives. It's my goal to inspire in you—the reader—a deeper discovery of your own existence.

However, I wouldn't have fulfilled my obligation in this book if I didn't submit my suggestion as to a way forward.

—✳—

This profound affirmation for a way forward should start with what got us here in the first place, which could be defined as the trivialization and ambivalent interpretation given to the omnipotent nature of love and acceptance. Acceptance and love are freely given by grace. You don't have to earn, apply for, or request grace, love, or acceptance, for they are all freely given as our inherent birthright, and we have no say so in the confirmation process. With acceptance, grace, and love as our birthright, why then have we and the church wandered so far away from these basic inalienable truths to arrive where we are?

I explained earlier that we have many interpretations of the Bible and will expound here since whether we wholly agree with it or not, it's part and parcel an integral part of our beliefs. Let's begin by exploring its historical advancement.

The Bible as we know it today came long after the literature it comprises. It is actually a group of books which includes the input of lots of different people. Their individual written materials were not intended to eventually become a part of a Bible. This may help explain a book of erotic love poetry (Song of Songs), a book that doesn't mention God (Esther), and a personal correspondence (Paul's letter to Philemon). It is also important to note that the King James Bible was born out of religious and political turmoil—and that none of it was written by Jesus or God.

If you read the English Bible like most of us do, you are reading a translation since the original Old Testament was written in Hebrew with the exception of a few Aramaic texts. The New Testament was originally written in Greek. Translation by its nature is interpretation and the translator has to make word choices. Even the Ten Commandments, which would seem to be an absolute, shows up in two different places in the Bible with differences. Truthfully speaking, not everyone who believes in the Bible even has or reads the same one.

The point I wish to make here is no matter what our beliefs are, they are often based largely on interpretations handed to us from others. Often they agree or disagree with our own inherent affirmation of truth but it is solely up to us to harness our own enlightenment and to embrace our own truth and awareness. We cannot entrust this divine birthright to others to decide for us. We must interpret for ourselves our distinct relationship with God and the only absolute that could be applied unequivocally to every individual interpretation in the universe is love.

We can live and exist without politics or religion, but we cannot without love. Love and compassion is a necessary part of human existence and survival. Everything in the higher realm of the universe operates this way. Clouds do not condemn the rain, or criticize other clouds. The forest does not demonize its trees, or rebuke new fallen seeds. It is only man who has difficulty in becoming one with nature and God. Why the incessant need to demonize, ostracize, and repudiate other creatures of an omnipotent God, and how can we again be one with God?

My assertion is that love—alone and unencumbered—will bridge these and every divide that has formed since the beginning of time, and every divide yet to come. It is paramount that our mind, soul, and spirit, above all, embrace the love you emanated from since the beginning. Love is the authority that allows us to pull anything we truly want from the celestial and mysterious realm of the universe.

Let's first understand that the nature of love includes all in existence. Unbelievably yet unmistakably, this limitless love was the root of the Christian faith. In order to remain faithful to love, we should be aware of the moral values established by others, but steadfastly hold our inner values paramount. This once-omnipresent love has now been trivialized, watered down, and given many different meanings to fit man's insistence on dividing and labeling others.

I've used many analogies in this book to explain that God, Love, Source, and Universe are all the same. It doesn't matter what you call it, or if you give it a name at all. It always remains constant and steadfast. It is in our egotistical attempts at self-serving behavior that we part from this truth. The moment we place conditions on our love, it is no longer unencumbered love but rather a perversion of love. As difficult as this may be too grasp for some, this law applies everywhere. With mindless complacency, we've embraced a watered-down version of love and God for many generations; we now accept that erroneous interpretation of love as truth and use it for our self-serving egos.

This erroneous interpretation has affected our entire society, both inside and outside of the religious environment. For us to say we have love without acceptance would be ridiculous. This is easiest to understand when it comes to spouses: if one doesn't accept one's spouse completely, authentic love is not present. If we don't accept others as they are, as perfect yet imperfect as they are, that "love" is selfish. Let's release the egotistical shackles of judging others or ourselves and begin experiencing the bliss of heaven right here and now.

Perfection and imperfection have to work in unity. Without one, the other could not exist. When we are constantly striving to remake others, then we are working against the natural laws of the universe that facilitate creation and destruction. Nature and our bodies work that way as well. Millions of cells each day die off to allow new cells to be created. Trees lose their branches and leaves, only to make way for new ones. In order to experience love, we need to embrace all that is, just the way it was intended.

The first chance you get to walk barefoot in the grass, do so, and appreciate the grass' acceptance and non-judgment. Count the stars at night and dwell for a moment in amazement at how connected (invisibly) we are to each of them. Perform unselfish acts of kindness for people who you view as strangers, and think kindly of even those you've not fully accepted yet and you will immediately begin to feel the bliss of your birthright and the Universe. That is what we're all here for: to love and accept each other, not to judge each other.

Unfortunately, society has only helped to foster our false sense of self, encouraging us to discriminate and separate. We created race, class, and intelligence distinctions that are irrelevant, or are not even existent. However, is is understandable that we might experience difficulty in accepting others, given that many of us don't even accept those we married, and are forever trying to change!

This rejuvenation of love must begin from the inside, with a conscious desire to love ourselves. Smile at yourself in the mirror. Say to yourself how wonderful and beautiful you are, as you are.

Despite an economic downturn in this country, Americans spent 12.4 billion dollars on plastic surgery in one year.[19] Breast augmentation, nose reshaping, eyelid surgery, liposuction, and tummy tucks were the most popular procedures. Might I suggest that we'd save money and resources if we would resist finding fault in the mirror? Take a look at ourselves with no make up, tired eyes, sagging skin, and soften our expectations a bit to enjoy our humanness. Let's accept our perceived imperfections and enjoy the road we're on, because who knows when it will end?

This journey begins at the core of the soul once more, and the judgments must cease. When we judge others even in the slightest, it doesn't reflect poorly on them—it serves to highlight our own lack

---

19   American Society of Plastic Surgeons

of acceptance. We only see the bad in others because our minds have contrasted that experience with something we have perceived as good and vice versa. If the sun never shone, we would know only darkness, and judgment would be irrelevant because there'd be no day to compare. There'd be no such thing as light, and night would not be considered good nor bad. It would be free from judgment.

We can easily see how all the preconceived notions and beliefs have taken a seemingly inexorable hold on our lives and our society. The road forward will not be a simple flipping of a master switch, for we must wholly revere our minds, which are our foremost connections to God, our Source, and the Universe.

When my cousin and I were both about ten years old, we would share any monies or things of value we had with each other. He was a lot more fortunate in that he'd constantly receive a lot more money than I ever would. When he'd end up with ten dollars that his mom had given him, he felt obliged to share it 50/50 with me, without a question or second thought. Those were our natural childhood instincts. Several years later, we had become accustomed to lack. We had learned, for shortsighted and selfish reasons, not to share as much. It's a curious wonder that those instinctive thoughts of abundance are still buried somewhere in our minds. How can we reactivate them?

It should be no surprise that our pilgrimage back to Source begins with us remembering whence we came, because if we don't know our Source, we certainly can't return to it. We all emanated from this Source's love and lost our way on this earthly journey by asking every passerby for our directions, when many of them did not know their own. Subsequently, we aimlessly wandered until apathy and complacency set in, and we fell into the depths of despair and lost our remembrance of our origin. We reluctantly settled for less than our inherited blissful birthright. We accepted the notion that to struggle, suffer, and do without is a badge of honor, and that we should be proud and await our reward elsewhere.

However, let me remind you that life is and should be beautiful and blissful right here and now. I cannot overstate the impact of creating your world with your own mind, and not that of someone else who may still maintain the dominance of your mind today. It could be someone in your past who may not even be around anymore, or someone today who has dominion and mastery over your mind. The power of your mind belongs to you and you alone, and I implore you not to squander it.

Don't let others seize the gift uniquely given to you to treasure. I encourage you to take the first step in this dance with God, and stop trying to be perfect and expecting perfection in others. See yourself in everyone, and everyone in you, because we are not as separate as we have been led to believe.

Practice accepting that vulnerable place within you and allowing others to see it as well. God loves us no matter what we've been told, and does not care about our trivial imperfections. That was the trade off in giving us free will. It's now up to us to surrender to the universe and receive this gift. Don't oppose love, but rather embrace and do what love asks of you. There is no need to fight with life or fret over our imperfections, for this disorderly chaos is working in perfect harmony with the rest of creation. Just get in the flow and enjoy this beautiful dance. If you don't get the steps just right at first, then continue the dance, and soon you will be moving gracefully to the rhythm of life and love.

Without imperfection there is no perfection. Remember that dying and destruction are part of the process for any living thing. Perfection along with imperfection are the integral parts of living and creating. Leaves die and fall off the tree, only to make room for new ones to grow.

Our skin cells are dying off every day, only to make room for new skin cells to form. It's how creation works. Not anything in nature—birds, trees, clouds and so on—frets over apparent imperfections, yet God continues to provide for and take care of all.

This awareness—in individuals and religious institutions alike—must start from within. The church can make a huge difference in the reconnection to God, because the church is already full of followers, eagerly awaiting guidance toward self-awareness! It's time for the church to admit its own shortcomings instead of pointing out others' shortcomings. The church has to humble itself to accept that there are many questions for which it does not yet have an answer, and just as many answers without questions to match.

When we humble the hearts and minds of men to appeal to our highest calling of love, we will see a momentous shift toward bettering all mankind. We must take back our minds if we're to get back to God and love. We cannot fault religion or the church for leading us on this path—we willingly pursued it. If we are not getting the answers we seek, then perhaps that is our wake-up call to seek another place, where we can begin within as opposed to without.

We no longer have to pretend we're invincible, or that we know all the answers. Just know that we are made up of the same stuff that make up stars, worlds, and galaxies. It was this Source that made you to be uniquely you and the stars to be stars, but all are one with this Source.

Love, forgiveness, peace, grace, happiness, and joy are your inalienable birthright. Don't judge or question it or wait on others to validate them for you. Just accept them, because they are yours exclusively when you mind your own life.

The book cover for The Great Gatsby, one of the most celebrated in American literature, was created before F. Scott Fitzgerald finished his manuscript. Fitzgerald insisted that his editor lock in the artist who had done the artwork in advance: "For Christ's sake, don't give anyone that jacket you're saving for me. I've written it into the book!"

The artwork so sparked Fitzgerald's imagination and creative process that he'd written its image, a pair of eyes "blue and gigantic, their irises are one yard high [that] look out of no face," into his book.

The image functioned as a unique collaboration between author and artist, and served as a symbol that drove Fitzgerald's story—a story that became a critique of the American Dream.

As for me, I was minding my own life one day when I became inspired to create the artwork for Mind Your Own Life. Only in my case, it was long before I ever knew there was a book.

As a Creative, I never question inspiration when it flows. It keeps me well. I know that my inspiration and intuition is a direct line to the Universe that created me. I tune in and pay attention when it makes itself known.

Oliver and Aaron were unaware that I had started working on a portrait of them in May 2010. Six months later, during one of our continuing conversations about the nature of existence, I learned that a book was in the works—one that shares Aaron's personal expression of a deeper order and spiritual awakening in his life. Aaron commented that things were moving along well with the manuscript, but that in one area he was completely stumped. "What to do about a book cover?" We were both surprised to hear me say, "oh . . . but I think you already have one!"

We laughed and accepted the discovery, as crazy as it seemed, that our paths had entwined. If a pair of floating eyes could drive the story in The Great Gatsby, were our two separate but synchronistic energies driving the cover? Neither one of us knew the other's intentions. Since I didn't know what the book was about, would the artwork, in one visual flash, speak for its meaning? It never crossed our minds.

I revealed the portrait to Oliver and Aaron in December 2010. In it, they appear iridescent and glowing, transcendental as they navigate the everyday, breathing in a measure of bliss while they make their own rules.

The cover drives the story home for all of us—that when you Mind Your Own Life and journey back to love, it comes from your soul.

Elizabeth Indianos
ElizabethIndianos.com